LET GO & LET GOD

A 40 Day Daily Devotional of the Promises of God

Let Go & Let God
A 40 Day Daily Devotional of the Promises of God

Copyright © 2025 by Marguerite Remy-Esannason

All rights reserved. No part of this book may be reproduced or transmitted in any form or by any means without written permission from the author.

Scriptures referenced: The Holy Bible, King James Version. New York: American Bible Society: 1999; Bartleby.com, 2000. New King James Version © 1982 by Thomas Nelson, Inc. All rights reserved. Used by permission.

Grace Greater Than Our Sin, Julia H. Johnston (1910) – Public Domain.

Great Is Thy Faithfulness, Thomas O. Chisholm (1923) – Public Domain.

"Worthy Is Your Name" by Elevation Worship. © 2018 Capitol CMG Paragon / Songs of Red Rocks / Bethel Music Publishing. Used by permission.

Definitions of "heritage" quoted from Merriam-Webster.com Dictionary. © Merriam-Webster, Incorporated. Accessed July 8, 2025. Used under fair use for educational purposes.

Cover Design by Diana Harris-Stewart

First Edition
ISBN: 979-8-9867151-4-8

10 9 8 7 6 5 4 3 2 1
Printed in the United States of America.

Book Design by:
STALEON® GROUP PUBLICATIONS
www.StaleonPublishing.com

The name Staleon is a registered trademark of Staleon Group Publications, LLC.

LET GO

LET GOD

A 40 Day Daily Devotional
of the Promises of God

MARGUERITE REMY-ESANNASON

Staleon Group
Publications
Orlando • Dallas

ALSO BY MARGUERITE REMY-ESANNASON

Soar With Wings Like Eagles
Soar With Wings Like Eagles, Volume 2

DEDICATION

The following people are greatly cherished and forever knitted into my heart. They have supported me, encouraged me, and pushed me to the finish line.

To Elder Harold Fuller, my dear friend, my Elder and partner in intercession. For your wise counsel and teaching of total trust and reliability on the Word of God, the Holy Bible, as being the only foundation of our life in Christ.

To Angela Lewis and Twana Jefferson, my two sisters in Christ, who always encourage me to exercise my gifts and serve as the hands of God extended in my life in more ways than one—thank you for recognizing what God has placed inside me and for being true gifts from God.

To Ethel Cooley, who inspired me to express God's faithfulness and goodness in my life—thank you for your encouragement and your labor of love in this project.

To Tera Dahl, my dear, faithful, and humble friend, whose expertise and strength have contributed to the excellence and prestige of this book.

A special acknowledgment to my spiritual mentor, Pastor Paula White-Cain, a giant in the faith, who continually contributes to my spiritual growth and maturity, and who stands as a powerful example of courage and faithfulness—even when standing alone against the odds.

TABLE OF CONTENTS

ALSO BY MARGUERITE REMY-ESANNASON v
DEDICATION vii
INTRODUCTION xi
WHY A "40-DAY" DEVOTIONAL xiii
DEVOTIONS 17
    A PLACE IN GOD 19
    BOLDNESS 21
    CHILDREN 23
    CONFIDENCE 25
    COURAGE 27
    DELIVERANCE 29
    FAITH 33
    FAITHFULNESS 35
    FAMILY 39
    FAVOR 43
    FEAR NOT 47
    FORGIVENESS 49
    GOD'S WORD 53
    GRACE 57
    HEALING 61
    HERITAGE 65
    HUMILITY 69
    LOVE 73
    MARRIAGE 77
    OBEDIENCE 81

PATIENCE	85
PEACE	89
PRAYER	91
PROMISE	95
PROSPERITY	97
PROTECTION	99
PURPOSE	103
RIGHTEOUSNESS	107
SALVATION	109
THANKSGIVING	113
THE FEAR OF THE LORD	117
THE JOY OF THE LORD	121
THE PERSON OF THE HOLY SPIRIT	125
TRUST	129
TRUTH	133
UNDERSTANDING	137
UNITY	139
VICTORY	143
WISDOM	145
WORSHIP GOD	149
ENDORSEMENTS	**153**
BY PASTOR PAULA WHITE-CAIN	153
BY REVEREND DR. PAUL ZAHL	155

INTRODUCTION

As I come of age, I recognize that for victory in the path of life, we must **"Let Go and Let God"**.

God has given us all things that pertain to life and godliness.

God always has a remnant—even if it's Noah and his family, even if it's one man called King David.

He only needs one person to demonstrate how faithful and true He is. How loving, forgiving, and compassionate He is. Be that person.

God knows the state of man. He knows our limitations. That's why He invites us to come to Him.

He is patient with us, even when we do not acknowledge Him. Only with His help can we live a successful and victorious life—not by man's standards or the world's, but by the supernatural power of God.

"Not by might, nor by power, but by My Spirit," says the Lord.

When we **Let Go and Let God**, our lives can truly be successful. We must believe in Him and walk in obedience to His Word. These devotional exhortations will help propel you, ignite your faith, and strengthen your relationship with God.

Marguerite Remy-Esannason

WHY A "40-DAY" DEVOTIONAL

What is the significance of the number 40 in the Bible?

A 40-Day Daily Devotional is spiritual medicine for finding Victory in the Path of Life.
It is Food for the Journey—40 days of sustenance for your walk with God.

In Scripture, the number 40 often symbolizes a period of testing, preparation, or spiritual transformation. It is a time of challenge that leads to growth and divine encounter.

Consider the following examples:

- The Israelites wandered in the wilderness for 40 years, a time of testing and preparation before entering the Promised Land.

- The flood in Noah's time lasted 40 days, cleansing the earth and ushering in a new covenant.

- Elijah's journey to Mount Horeb (1 Kings 19:8) took 40 days, sustained by a single meal provided by God.

- Nineveh was given 40 days to repent through the prophet Jonah—and they did!

- Jesus fasted and prayed in the wilderness for 40 days, preparing Him for His public ministry. He returned in the power of the Holy Spirit.

- After His resurrection, Jesus appeared to His disciples for 40 days, preparing them for their mission in the world.

- Moses spent 40 days and nights on Mount Sinai, encountering God and receiving the Ten Commandments.

Each of these 40-day periods ended in a new beginning, a divine breakthrough, or a life-altering shift.

In our culture, 30 days is often the standard timeframe:

"You have 30 days to respond."
"Offer expires in 30 days."
"Apply within 30 days."

But God gives us 10 more days. Why?

Because His timing is not our timing.
His ways are higher.
His schedule is better.

That's one reason for this 40-Day Devotional:
It sets us apart from the world's standard of "30."

It calls us to walk in God's timing, with hearts ready for transformation, breakthrough, and intimacy with Him.

Devotions

A PLACE IN GOD

Acts 17:28
"For in Him we live and move, and have our being; as certain also of your own poets have said, 'For we are also His offspring.'"

Understanding Our Place in God

Jesus taught in Scripture that when we need to be with God, we should *go into our closet and close the door*. Being with God in secret allows Him to reward us openly. However, this teaching also refers to something deeper—a place **IN** God, not just a place *with* God.

A place **IN** God is a spiritual state, whether you are alone or surrounded by others, where you have the security and assurance of being one with Him. It is the understanding that, as the Scripture teaches, *"In Him we live and move and have our being."*

Daniel in the lion's den found his place **IN** God. Shadrach, Meshach, and Abednego in the fiery furnace were protected because they were **IN** God. Paul and Silas, even in chains and imprisonment, existed in that place **IN** God. Their physical surroundings could not affect the security and peace they experienced spiritually.

There is a Place in God

There is a place in God:
A place of stillness and quietness,
A place to renew your strength,
To run and not grow weary, to walk and not faint.

There is a place, a special place,
A place of revelation, a place of truth,
A place of light, a place of life.
There is a place in God, flying with wings of eagles,
Soaring to new heights, above the cares and snares of this world,
Above the weights and sins that entangle us,
Above the walls, struggles, and hindrances of life.

A place of joy with pleasures evermore—
There is a place, a special place, a place **IN** God.

PRAYER

Heavenly Father, in the name of Jesus, I come before You, knowing that You receive me just as I am. I pray that I may find that place **IN** You—a place of peace, security, and divine connection. Almighty God, my Creator and Savior, I believe that with You all things are possible.

I pray for that sacred place **IN** You where we can never be separated—You in me and I in You.
A sacred place, a holy place, a secure place.
A place in God.

I receive it now, in Jesus's name. Amen.

Galatians 2:20
"I am crucified with Christ: nevertheless I live; yet not I, but Christ liveth in me: and the life which I now live in the flesh I live by the faith of the Son of God, who loved me, and gave Himself for me."

BOLDNESS

Ephesians 3:12
"In whom we have boldness and access with confidence by the faith of him."

Approaching God with Boldness

Hebrews 4:16 teaches, *"Let us therefore come boldly unto the throne of grace, that we may obtain mercy, and find grace to help in time of need."*

Just as Moses was called to approach Pharaoh and demand the release of the children of God—even at the risk of his own life—he walked with boldness and confidence because he knew God had spoken. In his flesh, he did not feel adequate enough to speak, but he brought Joshua with him, knowing that God is able to turn every situation around.

Walking in Boldness and Confidence

When we cast aside our fears, intimidation, and lack of faith, God invites us to come to Him boldly and with confidence. This kind of boldness is only possible when we know the Word of God concerning our situation. We can also walk in boldness when we are aware of God's will for our lives. We move with confidence when we have spent time in His presence, feeling His heart and understanding His mind.

Access Granted Through Jesus

We have been granted access into the throne room of God to enter with boldness. When Jesus died on the cross, the veil in the temple was torn from top to bottom, symbolizing unrestricted access to God's presence. Nothing can hold us back from approaching our Heavenly Father with boldness, confidence, and faith, knowing that He hears and answers our prayers.

PRAYER

Heavenly Father, I come boldly into Your throne of grace to obtain mercy and help in my time of need. I thank You for receiving me and hearing me. I thank You for granting me access into Your presence. I thank You that Jesus is making intercession for me right now.

I come against every obstacle, every restriction, and every limitation that would prevent me from stepping out in faith with boldness and confidence in You and what You have already spoken. I thank You for releasing the spirit of boldness in my life as I exercise faith in You and Your Word.

In Jesus's name, I pray. Amen.

Hebrews 13:6
"So that we may boldly say, 'The Lord is my helper, and I will not fear what man shall do unto me.'"

CHILDREN

Psalm 127:3
"Lo, children are a heritage of the LORD: and the fruit of the womb is his reward."

The Precious Gift of Children

Children are incredibly precious and meaningful in the sight of God. God sent His Son, Jesus Christ, into the world as a child to save mankind. Jesus even rebuked His disciples when they attempted to keep children away from His presence and ministry. God sends us into the world as children—with a plan, with a purpose—to live out our lives glorifying Him.

The Bible teaches that *children are a heritage of the Lord.* They are a reward from God Himself to parents. A heritage is something valuable that multiplies, extends, and impacts generations. In our lives, we must receive every child as a blessing from God, especially our own.

The Responsibility of Parents

The Bible instructs parents in **Ephesians 6:4**, *"Provoke not your children to wrath: but bring them up in the nurture and admonition of the Lord."* Despite any shortcomings our children may have, we are called to exercise the fruit of the Spirit in our lives. We are to be living examples, training our children so that the purpose God has destined for them will be fulfilled, impacting generations to come.

God entrusts parents with the profound responsibility of nurturing, guiding, and instilling godly principles in their children. When we invest love, discipline, and godly wisdom into their lives, we are sowing seeds that will bring forth a great harvest—one that will change and influence future generations.

PRAYER

Heavenly Father, in the name of Jesus, I thank You for every child You have sent into this world. I commit to doing everything in my power to preserve and protect the gift of life. From this day forward, I will see every child as a blessing from You and will receive them in Your Name, knowing that the seeds I plant in their lives will bring forth a great harvest. I believe these seeds will change and influence generations to come.

As Your Son Jesus changed the world, I pray that my investment in every child will change the world within their sphere of influence. In Jesus's name, I pray. Amen.

Colossians 3:20
"Children, obey your parents in all things: for this is well pleasing unto the Lord."

CONFIDENCE

Philippians 1:6
"Being confident of this very thing, that He which hath begun a good work in you will perform it until the day of Jesus Christ."

Our confidence in anything is directly related to the **investment, labor, and time** we have devoted to it. Giving our lives to Christ is the **best decision** we have ever made. Living for Christ is the **greatest investment** we can ever make because that decision carries **eternal rewards**.

God never fails, and placing our **confidence in Him**, putting our **trust in Him**, and above all, having **faith in Him** brings total assurance of **success—not failure**.

Our daily lives should reflect confidence in the **God who created the heavens and the earth** with the words of His mouth. Our daily lives should demonstrate confidence in the **God who never fails**. Our lives should be a testimony that **God has called us to Himself** by saving us through the finished work of **Jesus Christ His Son on Calvary**.

Today, we walk in confidence, knowing that the **God of heaven and earth** will **complete the work** He has begun in us. Despite our **shortcomings and failures**, He has promised **never to leave us nor forsake us**. He has vowed to **complete the work** He has started in our lives.

Today, make it your mission to **complete something you have started or have procrastinated about**. Ask God for His help before you begin the project or attempt to complete it.

PRAYER

Heavenly Father, in the name of Jesus, I confess **total confidence in You**, the **God of creation**. I place my **confidence and trust** in You—the **God who never fails**. I trust in the One who **calmed the storm** and **parted the sea** so that Your children could walk across on **dry land**. I place my **confidence** in the **God who sends fire from heaven**. I trust in the **God who fights my battles** and **contends with those who contend with me**.

I place total **confidence and trust** in the **God who has given His angels charge over me,** to keep me in all my ways. I trust in the **God who is the same yesterday, today, and forever**. I will not **cast away this confidence**, for You are **faithful to Your Word**.

Thank You, Father.
In Jesus' name, Amen.

Hebrews 10:35–36
"Cast not away therefore your confidence, which hath great recompense of reward. For ye have need of patience, that, after ye have done the will of God, ye might receive the promise."

COURAGE

Psalm 27:14
"Wait on the LORD: be of good courage, and he shall strengthen thine heart: wait, I say, on the LORD."

Courage Through Adversity

In life, we often face many obstacles—some real and some imagined. Challenges will undoubtedly cross our paths daily. **Proverbs 24:16** speaks of courage: *"For a just man falleth seven times, and riseth up again."* Courage is what empowers us to rise when we fall, despite the odds stacked against us.

Courage equips us to stand firm in the face of overwhelming challenges. To develop courage, we must weigh the benefits and disadvantages of our actions, make well-thought-out decisions, and move forward without second thoughts. Knowing God's will for your life will be accomplished as you walk before Him in truth.

Waiting on the Lord for Strength

Our courage grows as we wait upon the Lord and receive direction and instruction for the circumstances that surround us. This direction and instruction come from God's Holy Word. **Isaiah 55:11** declares, *"So shall my word be that goeth forth out of my mouth: it shall not return unto me void, but it shall accomplish that which I please, and it shall prosper in the thing whereto I sent it."*

The Word of God will accomplish what He has promised in your life. As we wait upon the Lord, our faith and courage are strengthened, enabling us to stand firm.

Our scripture text promises that as we wait upon the Lord and remain courageous, God Himself will strengthen our hearts. The courage and strength that God's Word imparts allow us to be strong and do great exploits—not in our own strength, but in the strength of the Lord.

PRAYER

Heavenly Father, today I wait on You. I cast my cares upon You and receive strength and courage through Your Word. Thank You for the promise that Your people shall be strong and do exploits. Today, I stand courageous in the face of any obstacle, any challenge, or any limitation that comes my way, because I know the God who lives inside of me is insurmountable, and nothing is too hard for You. As You are, so am I in this world. I give You thanks and praise for Your promises. In Jesus's name. Amen.

Daniel 11:32
"But the people that do know their God shall be strong, and do exploits."

DELIVERANCE

John 5:5–9

And a certain man was there, which had an infirmity thirty and eight years. When Jesus saw him lie, and knew that he had been now a long time in that case, he saith unto him, Wilt thou be made whole? The impotent man answered him, Sir, I have no man, when the water is troubled, to put me into the pool: but while I am coming, another steppeth down before me. Jesus saith unto him, Rise, take up thy bed, and walk. And immediately the man was made whole, and took up his bed, and walked: and on the same day was the sabbath.

A Lesson in Deliverance

This scripture passage teaches us a profound lesson about deliverance. The Bible does not mention the man's name, intentionally focusing not on his identity but on the act of deliverance for a man who had been bound for **38 years**, entirely dependent on others for help. He was stuck in a state of hopelessness, surrounded by people but receiving no assistance, even after nearly four decades.

This man did not only need healing in his body—he needed deliverance in his mind. His mindset had been conditioned to depend on people for help. Despite being surrounded by many, he remained neglected and alone in his suffering. Jesus, seeing him lying there, knew he had been in that condition for a long time. With a simple command, Jesus delivered him from the spirit of infirmity.

Jesus Sees You Today

Do you need help? Jesus sees your condition today. Look to Him for your deliverance. What is your situation right now? Jesus is asking you the same question He asked the man at the pool: "Wilt thou be made whole?" Ask Him, believe in Him, and He will do it.

Focus on the Healer, and you will receive healing. Concentrate on the Deliverer, and you will be delivered. Change your mindset today. Deliverance is yours—receive it.

Jesus taught His apostles in **John 16:33**: "In the world ye shall have tribulation: but be of good cheer; I have overcome the world." This means that whatever tribulation this world brings, we have already overcome because Jesus has made provision for our deliverance. Life may bring challenges, pain, sorrow, and afflictions, but God has already prepared a hope of deliverance in Him. Just as Jesus faced challenges in His earthly life, we, as His children, are not exempt from the trials of this world.

Walking in Faith and Deliverance

Our faith teaches us to walk by faith and not by sight—not by what we see, but by knowing that God will lift the burden and break the chains of affliction in our lives. Jesus demonstrated this principle when He spoke, "It is written," to counter every temptation and challenge. Likewise, we must declare, "It is written," concerning every situation we face.

The Word of God holds the antidote for every situation, whether it is health-related, family issues, business matters, or financial concerns. God's Word has a solution for each challenge. The Holy Spirit within us brings forth deliverance as we apply God's Word to our lives in obedience and declare it with faith.

PRAYER

Heavenly Father, in the name of Jesus, I receive deliverance in every area of my life. You promised in Your Word, "Many are the afflictions of the righteous: but the LORD delivereth him out of them all." I walk in deliverance because the Holy Spirit lives in me. I walk in deliverance because I obey Your Word. I walk in deliverance because Jesus purchased my freedom with His blood and took upon Himself all my sicknesses, diseases, and afflictions; therefore, I walk in divine health and healing.

I walk in deliverance in my spirit, soul, and body because I have given my life to You, and You live in me. I walk in deliverance because I serve You and my fellow man, walking in love toward those around me. I walk in deliverance because of Your mighty love and power. I walk in financial deliverance because I give, and You said, "It shall be given unto you, good measure, pressed down, shaken together, and running over."

I give You thanks and praise today and every day for my total deliverance. In Jesus's name. Amen.

Psalm 31:1–2
"In thee, O LORD, do I put my trust; let me never be ashamed: deliver me in thy righteousness. Bow down thine ear to me; deliver me speedily: be thou my strong rock, for an house of defense to save me."

FAITH

Romans 10:17
"So then faith cometh by hearing, and hearing by the word of God."

The Father of Faith

The Bible refers to Abraham as the "father of faith." He believed God even when what God promised seemed impossible. His faith was not just in what God said, but in Who God is—His character and His nature.

Did someone teach Abraham about God before God spoke to him? The Bible does not record any prior communication between them. Was he seeking God? Did Abraham recognize that there was a Supernatural Being orchestrating what was around him? Did he come to understand that there was more to life than mere survival? Was there a longing in his heart for more?

God must have seen that longing. He discerned that Abraham's heart was ready—ready to listen, ready to obey. His faith was already stirring, energized by a search for something greater. Abraham was dissatisfied with the status quo, and God saw a man He could use for His glory—a man who could give birth to a nation dedicated to Himself. Abraham was ready. He believed God and walked by faith, not knowing where he was going but remaining sensitive to the voice of God.

Developing Sensitivity to God's Voice

We can all develop that sensitivity to the voice of God. God is speaking continually—He speaks through His Word. Unlike Moses, Gideon, or Samson, who initially struggled to accept the Word of the Lord, we have the written Word of God to learn from and grow in faith.

We do not need great faith; we need faith as small as a mustard seed. I once bought a container of mustard seeds just to gauge the level of my faith against one of these tiny seeds. They are incredibly small—

almost too small to believe. Then the revelation struck me: it is not about what we see with our eyes but the level of trust and abandonment we have in what God says.

Faith in God's Word grows and becomes fulfilling as we prioritize reading, meditating on, and memorizing His promises. God's Word will grow your faith and bring healing into your life. Man's words are often spoken without thought or purpose, but every syllable in God's Word is intentional and powerful.

Isaiah 55:11 declares, *"So shall my word be that goeth forth out of my mouth: it shall not return unto me void, but it shall accomplish that which I please, and it shall prosper in the thing whereto I sent it."*

Hold tightly to this truth. Grab it with your heart by faith, and never let it go.

Prayer

Heavenly Father, I come to You in the name of Jesus. I believe that You are God, and there is no other besides You. In the name of Jesus, I ask for an increase in faith as I read and believe Your Word. I thank You that Your Word will accomplish everything You have promised in my life. I trust in the integrity of Your Word and its transformative power to grow my faith more and more.

I thank You that as I exercise my faith, You are pleased. Like Abraham, I will walk by faith and not by sight, inheriting Your promises. Thank You for the provision You have made for us all to receive Your Word and live by faith. I praise and thank You in Jesus's mighty name. Amen.

Hebrews 11:6
"But without faith it is impossible to please him: for he that cometh to God must believe that he is, and that he is a rewarder of them that diligently seek him."

FAITHFULNESS

Lamentations 3:22–23
"It is of the LORD'S mercies that we are not consumed, because his compassions fail not. They are new every morning: great is thy faithfulness."

It is because of the Lord's mercies that we are not consumed, for His compassions never fail.

Why?

Because He is faithful. God keeps His oaths, His vows, His Word, and His covenant.

The Faithful God

God declares, *"I am a covenant-keeping God."* You are alive not because you have done anything to merit deliverance or have the strength to work your way out of your problems, but because of **My character**.

I am faithful. I am the everlasting God. I keep My Word. I say what I mean, and I mean what I say.

I give My Word. I have a plan. I do not change My plan because you missed it. I stick to My plan in spite of you or what you do.

I am faithful.

God has promised that when we obey Him, He will reward us up to a thousand generations. He is with us—and with those after us—for the long haul.

For the most part, we do not merit or deserve anything good in this world. We came into this life with breath and nothing else.

We were sent into this world with a plan and a purpose from God, and as we cooperate with Him, He makes things happen.

He promises never to leave us nor forsake us.

FAITHFULNESS!

The Definition of Faithfulness

Faithfulness is defined as *"The quality of being faithful, fidelity, loyalty, and consistency."* How many people have we disappointed? How many times have we failed to live up to our word or our commitments?

Faithfulness is a virtue that could transform the world if we put it into action.

Faithfulness is synonymous with God—the only truly faithful Being. We often allow feelings and attitudes to control us, meaning we are not always faithful. We sometimes fail to deny ourselves and demonstrate the love and care reflective of children of the **Faithful One.**

A Song of Faithfulness

The songwriter Thomas Obadiah Chisholm, though often sickly and fragile, wrote:

"Great is Thy Faithfulness, Great is Thy Faithfulness,
Morning by Morning New mercies I see,
All I have needed Thy Hand hath provided,
Great is Thy Faithfulness, Lord, unto me."

("Great is Thy faithfulness, Lord, unto me…" (Chisholm 1923).)

He recognized that no matter what was happening around him, he could see and experience God's faithfulness and love. Despite his physical limitations, he knew God was working in his life, and that presence was so overwhelming that it overshadowed his frailty.

Can You See God's Faithfulness?

You may have experienced a great loss or tragedy in your life, but even in that pain, can you recognize and declare God's faithfulness? Today is a good day to start. As the old hymn goes:

*"Count your blessings, name them one by one,
Count your blessings, see what God has done.
Count your blessings, name them one by one,
And it will surprise you what the Lord has done."*

HE IS FAITHFUL!

PRAYER

Heavenly Father, I thank You in Jesus's name for Your faithfulness. Though the earth be removed and cast into the seas, **You are faithful**. I thank You that when everything around me is changing, **You do not change**.

You are God. You change not. You are the same yesterday, today, and forever. You are faithful to the very end.

I thank You, even when I do not understand, I place my faith and trust in You, knowing that You are faithful in every situation that confronts me.
I pray in the name of Jesus that I will be faithful in all I put my heart and mind to so that others around me can depend on me to be Your faithful servant.

In Jesus's name, I thank You that the work You have begun in me, You will complete because of Your faithfulness.

Amen.

Deuteronomy 7:8–9
8. "But because the LORD loved you, and because he would keep the oath which he had sworn unto your fathers, hath the LORD brought you out with a mighty hand, and redeemed you out of the house of bondmen, from the hand of Pharaoh king of Egypt. 9. Know therefore that the LORD thy God, he is God, the faithful God, which keepeth covenant and mercy with them that love him and

keep his commandments to a thousand generations."

FAMILY

Genesis 2:15–18, 21–25
And the LORD God took the man, and put him into the garden of Eden to dress it and to keep it. And the LORD God commanded the man, saying, Of every tree of the garden thou mayest freely eat: But of the tree of the knowledge of good and evil, thou shalt not eat of it: for in the day that thou eatest thereof thou shalt surely die. And the LORD God said, It is not good that the man should be alone; I will make him an help meet for him.

And the rib, which the LORD God had taken from man, made he a woman, and brought her unto the man. And Adam said, This is now bone of my bones, and flesh of my flesh: she shall be called Woman, because she was taken out of Man. Therefore shall a man leave his father and his mother, and shall cleave unto his wife: and they shall be one flesh.

From the very beginning, in the Garden of Eden, God created man and woman and gave them to each other. He also set a precedent in verse 24, even though Adam and Eve did not have a physical mother or father present. God declared them to be **one**—one family, united as a single unit.

When God gave His creation the command to **multiply and replenish the earth**, this command was also extended to Adam and Eve. They were expected to start their own family, united as one. **One family. One unit.**

But from the very beginning, the enemy devised a plan to separate and divide what God had created. A plan to distort and challenge what God truly intended.

Family is particularly important to God because it demonstrates strength and unity. The family is the backbone of a community and a nation. Since the beginning of time, families have faced division and conflict. The enemy has not ceased in his attempts to disrupt what God cherishes so deeply—**unity and peace** within the family.

God established the man as the **head of the household** and the woman as his **helpmeet** and support. He entrusted parents with the role of nurturing and developing children who would grow up, start their own families, and establish a legacy on the earth.

In the New Testament, Ephesians 5:21–25, God provides specific instructions for His model of the family:

- The **husband's role** is to **love his wife as Christ loved the church** and gave His life for it.
- The **wife's role** is to **submit to, respect, and honor her husband.**
- The **children's role** is to **walk in obedience to their parents.**

This is God's design—a model that cannot be changed, altered, or bypassed for a successful family. Unfortunately, society has strayed from God's blueprint, resulting in the breakdown of families, communities, and even nations.

PRAYER

Heavenly Father, in the name of Jesus, I thank You for establishing the family unit according to Your divine order.

Father, as You have ordained the husband to be the head of the family, I pray that every man will take his rightful place, just as Jesus did as the Head of the Church. I pray that every man will love and cherish his wife.

Father, I ask that every wife will submit to her husband, honoring and respecting him as the head of the household. May she be his strong support and cling to him as one.

I pray that husbands and wives will train and bring up their children in the fear and admonition of the Lord. May parents be living examples to their children in both word and action.

I pray that the family unit will honor You and walk in obedience to Your Word. May they serve You wholeheartedly and be witnesses in their communities and nations.

I thank You and praise You for all that You have done and all that You will continue to do. In Jesus's mighty name, **Amen.**

Ephesians 5:21–25
Submitting yourselves one to another in the fear of God. Wives, submit yourselves unto your own husbands, as unto the Lord. For the husband is the head of the wife, even as Christ is the head of the church: and he is the saviour of the body. Therefore, as the church is subject unto Christ, so let the wives be to their own husbands in everything. Husbands, love your wives, even as Christ also loved the church, and gave himself for it.

FAVOR

Psalm 5:12
For thou, LORD, wilt bless the righteous; with favour wilt thou compass him as with a shield.

God surrounds the righteous with **favor**. But does favor depend on the condition of our hearts or our attitudes? Do we have any part to play in activating favor in our lives? Is there a specific instruction or principle that triggers favor?

Is right thinking and pleasing God a prerequisite for favor? He promises His children who walk in right standing with Him that they will be **the head and not the tail**. Is that not a promise of favor? God's favor surrounds us like a shield—a life of security and divine protection.

Consider Elijah during the famine. Why did he choose that **one woman with her son** to ask for a cake before she prepared it for herself and her son? Why not someone in the community who had more resources? Why her? Was it divine favor so that she would not perish during the famine? Was it favor that ensured she and her son would be provided for, even when those around her went hungry?

The Bible speaks of the Prophet Samuel, Queen Esther, Mary, and Jesus—all of whom found **favor** in the sight of God and man.

Why would someone with less education be promoted over someone with better credentials and more experience? Why would an employer bypass others and give a promotion to that specific person? Could that be **favor**?

Why would a person with less cash be approved for the purchase of a home over someone who could pay in full upfront?

We might not always **feel** the favor of God, but others can often see it clearly. Sometimes, we are so caught up in our circumstances that we fail to recognize God's favor working in our lives. Ask God to open your eyes so you can **see and feel** His favor in your life.

PRAYER

Heavenly Father, in the name of Jesus, I give You thanks and praise for the great and precious promises You have made to Your children. I thank You for Your presence being so real in my life as I open my mouth with praise and thanksgiving for who You are and what You have done.

Today, in the name of Jesus, I pray that Your **favor surrounds me as with a shield**. I ask You to release Your favor in every area of my life. May my eyes be opened to see the workings of Your favor in my life.

Father, may I walk worthy of Your favor as I interact with my brothers and sisters. I pray that You continue to work Your favor in my life so that I will walk in safety and security in You.

For all these things, I thank and praise You, Father, in Jesus's name. **Amen.**

Luke 2:52
And Jesus increased in wisdom and stature, and in favour with God and man.

FEAR NOT

Deuteronomy 31:6
Be strong and of a good courage, fear not, nor be afraid of them: for the LORD thy God, He it is that doth go with thee; He will not fail thee, nor forsake thee.

It is said that there are **365 references** in God's Word instructing us to *"fear not."* This daily reminder emphasizes the importance of walking each day without fear. Fear is the opposite of faith. God is highlighting that we should not walk in fear but in the **liberty** with which He has made us **free and fearless**.

As children of God, we should not walk in fear. We should have the assurance that God watches over His Word to perform it. But how do we come to believe what someone says? It is because we have built a **relationship** with that person, developing **faith and trust** over time.

To believe what God's Word says about *not fearing*, we must build a strong relationship with Him so that we can **believe** and **trust** in His promises.

David did not fear the **lion**, the **bear**, or the **giant Goliath**. Why? Because of his relationship with God and the experiences he had of God's **faithfulness** and **love**. He saw God deliver him before, and he trusted that God would do it again.

Fear affects not only our mental state but also our physical health. Fear governs both the **mental** and **physical** operations of our bodies, restricting the free function of our **circulatory** and **nervous systems**. It limits our movements, controls behavioral changes, and contributes to depressive-like behaviors.

1 Kings 19:11–13
And he said, Go forth, and stand upon the mount before the LORD. And, behold, the LORD passed by, and a great and strong wind rent the mountains, and brake in pieces the rocks before the LORD; but the LORD was not in the wind: and after the wind an earthquake; but the LORD was not in the

earthquake: And after the earthquake a fire; but the LORD *was not in the fire: and after the fire a still small voice. And it was so, when Elijah heard it, that he wrapped his face in his mantle, and went out, and stood in the entering in of the cave. And, behold, there came a voice unto him, and said, What doest thou here, Elijah?*

Even Elijah had to learn that God's presence is often in the *still small voice*, not always in the grand or dramatic. We must rise above fear by **trusting** and **believing** God in the small things, building our confidence in what He has said He will do.

PRAYER

Heavenly Father, today I trust in the integrity of Your Word. You have instructed us to *"fear not."* Today, I lay all my fears at Your feet and yield to Your love and faithfulness, knowing that what You have promised, You will perform. I build my faith and cast out fear by studying Your Word daily, for faith comes by hearing the Word of God, and Your perfect love casts out all fear. I will *"fear not"* because I know You are with me, You will strengthen me, and You will never leave nor forsake me.

In Jesus's name, I give You thanks and praise.
Amen.

2 Timothy 1:7
For God hath not given us the spirit of fear; but of power, and of love, and of a sound mind.

FORGIVENESS

1 John 1:9
"If we confess our sins, He is faithful and just to forgive us our sins, and to cleanse us from all unrighteousness."

The Promise of Forgiveness

God has given us great and precious promises that, if we believe and receive His Word, we can live a victorious life.

The Bible teaches that *all have sinned and fall short of the glory of God.* None of us can deny this truth. No one teaches a one-year-old to steal, yet the residue and impulse of Adam and Eve's sin resonate in every human being born into this world.

Understanding Forgiveness

Our topic today, *forgiveness,* is simple to understand but sometimes challenging to practice. This is especially true when we allow guilt and unforgiveness to dominate our thoughts, instead of letting God's Word renew our minds.

Psalm 103:12 assures us of God's forgiveness:
"As far as the east is from the west, so far has He removed our transgressions from us."

God promises to remove our sins and wrongdoings as far as the east is from the west. What a powerful and vivid image.

Confessed Sins Are Gone Forever

Confessed sins are erased and can never revisit your life—unless you allow the enemy to bring them back into your thoughts over and over again. *The east can never meet the west.* That is how far God has removed your sins.

Jesus emphasized the importance of forgiveness when He taught us to pray:

"Forgive us our trespasses as we forgive those who trespass against us."

We would not want God to hold any sin or transgression against us, so we must practice what Jesus taught: *forgive others in the same measure we expect God to forgive us.*

The Weight of Unforgiveness

Unforgiveness is like carrying a heavy load on your back day and night. Over time, it takes a toll on your physical, mental, and emotional health.

As far as I can see, there is no one and nothing important enough to forfeit the freedom, liberty, and peace that come with forgiveness.

Forgiveness is a Choice

Forgiveness is a personal decision. It is not based on feelings or whether the person accepts your forgiveness. It is a release from wrongdoing and a commitment not to speak negatively about the situation again.

Forgiveness is seeing Jesus hanging on the cross, His life draining from His body, yet He asks the Heavenly Father to forgive those who committed such an unjust and undeserved act that cost Him His life.

The Freedom of Forgiveness

Forgiveness is freedom.

- It is like taking wings and soaring.
- It is like a child, unburdened and free from unnecessary weights.
- It is a release that brings lightness and peace.

Though the act of forgiveness may be difficult, the freedom and liberty that follow are incomparable and deeply gratifying.

PRAYER

Heavenly Father, in the name of Jesus, I give You thanks and praise for the provision of forgiveness that You have made available to us, Your children. You gave Your only begotten Son to take our place so that the guilt and consequences of sin would not fall upon us but upon Him.

I receive Your forgiveness today. Father, I purpose in my heart that I too will walk in forgiveness and newness of life.

I make the quality decision today to release anyone in my life who has disappointed, used, or abused me. I cast all caution to the wind and freely release myself from any unforgiveness I may have been holding in my heart, whether consciously or unconsciously.
I cleanse myself with the blood of Jesus, and I walk in the liberty where You have made me free. Just as You forgive, I purpose in my heart to forgive each and every day that I live.
In Jesus's name, I pray. Amen.

Luke 6:37
"Judge not, and you shall not be judged; condemn not, and you shall not be condemned; forgive, and you shall be forgiven."

GOD'S WORD

2 Timothy 3:16
"All Scripture is given by inspiration of God, and is profitable for doctrine, for reproof, for correction, for instruction in righteousness."

Seeing the Bible as God's Voice

When you open the Bible, do you see it as God speaking directly to you? Or do you see it merely as a history book? Until you change your perspective of what the Bible truly is and *who* it is from, your life may remain mundane and unfulfilled.

The Holy Bible, as it is often called, was inspired by God and given to men to record, declaring His heart and His will for His people.

Isaiah 55:10-11 says:
"For as the rain comes down, and the snow from heaven, and do not return there, but water the earth and make it bring forth and bud, that it may give seed to the sower and bread to the eater, so shall My word be that goes forth from My mouth; it shall not return to Me void, but it shall accomplish what I please, and it shall prosper in the thing for which I sent it."

When you take the Word of God literally, apply it to your heart, and walk in obedience to its instructions, you will discover that the words on the pages are real—just as real as anything you can see with your eyes. The Word of God, when taken literally, will bring life and transform any situation.

God Honours His Word Above His Name

In **Psalm 138:2**, it is written:
"I will worship toward Your holy temple, and praise Your name for Your lovingkindness and Your truth; for You have magnified Your word above all Your name."

This passage declares that God places and honors His Word even above His own name. The name of God—Almighty, All-powerful, the Great I Am—is indeed mighty, yet He tells us, *"My Word is above My name."*

God defends His Word. He esteems it as more real than anything we can say about Him and more tangible than anything we can see—even the sun, moon, stars, and all of creation. He speaks, and it happens because His Word is powerful and unchanging.

Accepting God's Word as Truth

If you do not take the Word of God as *truth*—the only truth—then its reality and magnitude will never impact your life.

God declares that everything He has spoken will come to pass, whether we believe it or not. My encouragement to you is to *believe God*. My encouragement is to trust in God's Word.

Start with baby steps: choose a promise from God's Word that speaks to your situation. Apply that Word diligently and faithfully, speaking it over your life. You will begin to see real change—tangible, undeniable change. As real transformation occurs, your life will be revolutionized, and that change will affect not only you but also the lives of those around you.

The Word of God Transforms

Take the Word of God as truth. Let it dispel your doubts and fears. Apply it to your heart, renew your mind with it, and watch as your life changes for the better. This truth is too real and too powerful to ignore.

Make this world a better place for yourself and your loved ones. Make God's Word *your* words, and you will never be the same.

PRAYER

Heavenly Father, in the name of Jesus, I make the quality decision to believe that the Holy Bible is Your Word—Your Word of truth. I pray that the truth of Your Word dispels all my fears and doubts.

As I read Your Word, may faith arise in my heart, for faith comes by hearing and hearing by the Word of God. I thank You that as I daily read, meditate on, and study Your Word, my life will be transformed.

I pray that this world will be a better place because I believe in You and Your Word. I believe that man shall not live by bread alone but by every word that comes from Your mouth.

Today, I dedicate my life to taking Your Word seriously and witnessing the manifestation of Your promises in my life. Thank You for the provision You have made available to us, Your children, in Your Word.

In Jesus's name. Amen.

Hebrews 4:12
"For the word of God is living and powerful, and sharper than any two-edged sword, piercing even to the division of soul and spirit, and of joints and marrow, and is a discerner of the thoughts and intents of the heart."

GRACE

Psalm 84:11
"For the Lord God is a sun and shield; the Lord will give grace and glory; no good thing will He withhold from those who walk uprightly."

The Power and Gift of Grace

The songwriter beautifully declares:
*"Grace, Grace, God's grace,
Grace that will pardon and cleanse within,
Grace, Grace, God's grace,
Grace that is greater than all our sin."*

("Grace Greater Than Our Sin," Johnston, 1910)

This is a profound revelation of truth. It speaks to the grace of God, which reconciles us to Him. The blood of Jesus cleanses us from all our sins and restores us to fellowship with God. But it is the *grace of God* that keeps us covered.

It is God's grace that maintains our unity and keeps us under the care of the Almighty. Grace is the unmerited favor of God—something we did not earn and do not deserve.

Grace in Our Lives

Grace reveals the love of God that looks beyond our faults and sins to see the needs in our lives. Because of this, God extends grace— His unmerited favor—to help us move forward in the right direction. Even when we stumble or fail as children of God, His grace never leaves us.

It is the grace of God that enables us to stand strong during times of adversity and challenge.

Our Scripture text confirms:
"The Lord will give grace and glory; no good thing will He withhold from those

who walk uprightly." (Psalms 84:11, NKJV)

In our walk with God, His grace is ever-present. It never fails to cover us, strengthen us, and draw us closer to Him. The grace of God allows us to see Him as He truly is—in His power and His glory.

Never Take Grace for Granted

We should never take the grace of God for granted. Understanding that grace is something unearned and freely given should inspire us to walk humbly and meekly in obedience to God.

If grace were ever lifted from our lives, we would be left walking in darkness and without hope in this world.

A Parent's Grace as a Reflection of God's Grace

Think of your own son or daughter who may have disobeyed your instructions. Even though they may have acted wrongly, you extend grace to them because you love them.

You do not automatically cut them out of your life because of their mistakes. Your love and grace sustain the relationship with your children.

In the same way, our Heavenly Father's love and grace sustain us and keep us in relationship with Him. His grace is what covers our shortcomings and keeps us close to His heart.

PRAYER

Heavenly Father, in the name of Jesus, I thank You for the provision You have made to keep me close to Your heart and under Your care. I thank You for Your grace—that unmerited favor that You shower upon my life. It is a free gift, not something I earned or deserved, yet You extend it to me.

Thank You for accepting me as Your own, for shielding me, and covering me with Your grace. I praise You for the grace that is upon my life, drawing me closer to You.

Help me to extend that same grace and favor to my fellow man. In Jesus's name, I pray. Amen.

Acts 4:33
"And with great power, the apostles gave witness to the resurrection of the Lord Jesus, and great grace was upon them all."

HEALING

Matthew 9:35
"And Jesus went about all the cities and villages, teaching in their synagogues, preaching the gospel of the kingdom, and healing every sickness and every disease among the people."

The Question of Healing

A common question arises when Christians pass away due to illness: *"Why did God not heal this Christian? They served in the church, they did so much good, yet they were sick and died."*

Scripture teaches that God has already made provision for the healing of not only our spirits and souls but also our physical bodies.

Acts 10:38 tells us:
"How God anointed Jesus of Nazareth with the Holy Ghost and with power, who went about doing good and healing all who were oppressed by the devil, for God was with Him."

There are many examples and testimonies of people who have been healed from various sicknesses and diseases at different stages of life. The question remains: *Why are some healed and not others?*

Aspects of Healthy Living

Our bodies are the temple of the Holy Spirit, and the Holy Spirit lives within us. There is an order and responsibility in taking care of our physical bodies. If we abuse our bodies through poor decisions, there are natural consequences that follow.

Our habits significantly impact our health.

- What healthy habits have we incorporated into our daily lives?
- Are we eating the right foods?
- Are we engaging in physical exercise?
- Are we getting adequate rest?

Just like any living organism, our bodies require proper treatment to function effectively and serve us well throughout our lifetime.

The Power of Words

Another crucial aspect of healthy living is the words we speak. **Proverbs 18:21** teaches:
"Death and life are in the power of the tongue, and those who love it will eat its fruit."

Have the words we spoken concerning our health aligned with the Word of God?

- Have we been speaking negatively about our bodies?
- Have we been caring for our bodies with enough rest and proper nutrition?
- Are we following a healthy lifestyle that supports our well-being?

The Holy Sacrament of Communion

In the Holy Sacrament of Communion, Scripture warns that if we partake of the Body and Blood of Jesus unworthily—without examining ourselves—we may experience sickness or even death.

The Body and Blood of Jesus are sacred and holy, and God expects us to discern their significance as we partake of them. Provision has been made for the forgiveness of sins and cleansing through the sacrifice of Jesus on the cross. This means there is no excuse for receiving Communion unworthily.

God calls us to examine ourselves, to forgive others without limitation, for in the same measure we forgive, He forgives us.

Healing as God's Provision

Healing is God's provision for divine health for all mankind—not only for those who know Him but also for those who do not. Jesus took upon Himself the stripes on His back so that we might be healed.

Isaiah 53:5 reminds us:
"But He was wounded for our transgressions, He was bruised for our iniquities; the chastisement of our peace was upon Him, and by His stripes we are healed."

When we are afflicted or suffering from illness, we must remember that God has also granted wisdom to men, and science has advanced tremendously in providing relief for sickness and disease. Ultimately, God expects us to seek Him first in everything—including our health and healing.

The Role of the Holy Spirit in Healing

The Holy Spirit will guide us as we seek God's face concerning our individual health and healing. God answers prayer. He promises healing by the stripes of Jesus, and that promise is available to us as children of God.

When we pray, we must believe we receive, and we shall have it.

Mark 11:24 says:
"Therefore I say unto you, whatever things you desire when you pray, believe that you receive them, and you shall have them."

PRAYER FOR HEALING

Heavenly Father, I thank You for the provision You have made for bringing health and healing to our bodies. Jesus took upon Himself all my sicknesses, all my infirmities, and all my diseases, and with His stripes, I am healed.

I thank You for confirming in Your Word how Jesus went everywhere healing those who were sick and oppressed by the devil. There was not one person He turned away who was in need of healing.

I pray today, in the name of Jesus, that Your healing power be activated in my life. Let divine healing flow from the crown of my head to the soles of my feet. I give You thanks and praise for bringing wholeness to my spirit, soul, and body.

In the mighty name of Jesus, the Great Physician, I pray. Amen.

3 John 2
"Beloved, I pray that you may prosper in all things and be in health, just as your soul prospers."

HERITAGE

Proverbs 13:22
"A good man leaves an inheritance to his children's children, and the wealth of the sinner is laid up for the just."

The Meaning of Heritage

Webster's Dictionary defines *heritage* as:
- Property that is or may be inherited; an inheritance.
- A special or individual possession; an allotted portion.
- Something transmitted by or acquired from a predecessor; a legacy.

(Merriam-Webster. (n.d.). *Heritage*. In *Merriam-Webster.com dictionary*. Retrieved July 8, 2025, from https://www.merriam-webster.com/dictionary/heritage)

A heritage is something we receive freely—at no cost to the recipient.

Our Heritage as Children of God

What is our heritage as children of God? Are there tangible benefits to being a child of God and walking in His purposes and His will for our lives?

Scripture declares that a woman does not forget the child of her womb. She remembers the toil and pain of giving birth. Amid the joys of motherhood, she never forgets the experience of her child's birth.

God's Love and Our Inheritance

Is our Heavenly Father's love any less than that of a mother? While we were separated from God—not by our own doing, but because of the disobedience of our ancestor Adam—God was already planning for our salvation. He was planning for our *inheritance*.

Even while we were separated from Him, His thoughts were full of us, working out a plan to reconcile humanity back to Himself.

Did Jesus come to this earth, die for our sins, redeem us from the curse of sickness, poverty, and death, only to leave us abandoned? *Absolutely not.*

As children of God, we have a secure heritage—one that is destined for us both in this life and in the life to come. God has left us *benefits*. He has given us an *inheritance*. As His children, we automatically become heirs in the Kingdom of God and joint heirs with Jesus, the begotten of the Father.

Glory Through Suffering

Even as we go through life—enduring suffering, pain, and disappointment—Scripture teaches us that just as Jesus was glorified, we too shall be glorified with Him. The victory He purchased for us is our *heritage*.

Jesus Himself declared, *"There is no one good but One, that is, God."* If earthly men can leave an inheritance for their children and grandchildren, how much more would our Heavenly Father provide for His children?

The Wealth of Inheritance

Some of the wealthiest people in the world are those who have received an inheritance from parents, relatives, or even from people they never met. This happens because the recipients are entitled—whether as blood relatives, next of kin, or due to acts of kindness.

Our Inheritance in Christ

Our inheritance was purchased at Calvary, where Jesus shed His blood and redeemed us—spirit, soul, and body. Our heritage as children of God is secure.

God is a *covenant-keeping* God. He has already secured our inheritance, signed, sealed, and delivered with the blood of Jesus Christ.

PRAYER

Heavenly Father, I thank You for the provision You have made for Your children. Today, I walk in the liberty and confidence that all You have promised will come to pass.

I live as a joint heir with Christ, both in this world and in the world to come—in a glorious resurrection. Today, I am secure and walk in freedom, knowing that my inheritance is assured. What You have destined for my life, no one can take from me.

I thank You for the promise Jesus gave in **Mark 10:29-30**:
"Verily I say unto you, there is no man that hath left house, or brethren, or sisters, or father, or mother, or wife, or children, or lands, for My sake and the gospel's, but he shall receive a hundredfold now in this time—houses, and brethren, and sisters, and mothers, and children, and lands, with persecutions; and in the world to come, eternal life."

Thank You for the promise of Your Word.

In Jesus's name. Amen.

Isaiah 49:15-16
"Can a woman forget her nursing child, that she should not have compassion on the son of her womb? Yea, they may forget, yet I will not forget thee. Behold, I have graven thee upon the palms of My hands; thy walls are continually before Me."

HUMILITY

Matthew 23:11-12
"But he that is greatest among you shall be your servant. And whosoever shall exalt himself shall be abased; and he that shall humble himself shall be exalted."

The Definition of Humility

Webster defines *humility* as a virtue. It is the quality of being humble. Dictionary definitions describe humility as a sense of low self-regard and an awareness of one's own limitations. In a religious context, humility can mean recognizing one's position in relation to a deity (i.e., God) and submitting to that deity as part of one's faith.

Humility is defined as *"the state of being humble."* The word *humble* is often used to describe something or someone considered lowly or modest. For example, when someone refers to themselves as "just a humble editor" or speaks of their home as a "humble abode," they are indicating modesty and a lack of grandiosity.

Humility from a Christian Perspective

For Christians, *humility* is about staying in your place of assignment. It is not about rushing into what does not belong to you or striving for a position that is not yet yours. It means not thinking or acting above your current place in life. It means not elevating yourself above others—neither in words nor in actions—but being satisfied and at peace with your present state.

Humility demonstrates gratitude and appreciation for God's blessings and provisions in our lives. Because God is supreme, the Maker and Ruler of all things, humility is a sign of contentment and trust in His timing. It reflects a willingness to wait for His promotion when He sees fit.

Humility in Relationships and Community

Humility also enables us to walk in harmony with those around us. It allows others to achieve their personal goals while contributing to the greater good of the community.

Humility is a virtue that benefits not only the individual but also the community. It fosters a sense of unity, togetherness, and cooperation. So much more can be achieved when communities work together in humility rather than seeking personal gain and self-promotion.

The Contrast of Pride

The opposite of humility is *pride*. I see pride as rushing up a ladder without first checking its stability or safety, in an attempt to showcase a position that one is not prepared for. Eventually, as with all pride, there is a fall—and often, a painful one.

An Example of Humility: Mother Teresa

Mother Teresa (1910–1997) is a powerful example of humility. She was a Roman Catholic nun who devoted her life to serving the poor and destitute around the world. At a young age, she felt called to become a nun and serve the poor. At 18, she joined a group of nuns in Ireland, the Sisters of Loreto, and after a few months of training, she was sent to India.

Mother Teresa believed that serving others was a fundamental principle of Jesus Christ's teachings. She often referenced the words of Jesus and did not consider her own status or position. Instead, she humbled herself, prioritizing the needs of others above her own comfort or prestige.

She served the destitute, the poor, and the needy—those left to die on the side of the road—seeing in them their God-given dignity. Mother Teresa could have remained a sheltered nun, protected from the harsh realities of life. Yet she chose to make herself of *no reputation* and humbly served those less fortunate.

Her life is a reflection of the example Jesus set for us: coming to earth, making Himself of no reputation, and taking our place to save us.

PRAYER

Heavenly Father, in the name of Jesus, I give You thanks and praise for all You have given us as Your children. I thank You for the plan of salvation and for sending the Lord Jesus Christ into this world to reconcile us to Yourself.

Lord Jesus, You are the only begotten Son of the Father. Though You had Your place in heaven, You humbled Yourself and came to earth, making Yourself of no reputation. You humbled Yourself as a man to accomplish the greatest assignment ever attained by one person.

I pray, in the name of Jesus, that the same spirit of humility will lead and direct me as I live my life. I pray that the world will benefit because of my sensitivity to the needs and purposes of those around me.

Thank You for the work of the Holy Spirit in my life, who leads and guides me in fulfilling the greatest commandment: *"Love your neighbor as yourself."*

I purpose in my heart to walk humbly before You, to walk humbly before my fellow man, and to be honest with myself for the benefit of humanity.
In Jesus's name, I pray. Amen.

James 4:10
"Humble yourselves in the sight of the Lord, and He shall lift you up."

LOVE

John 3:16
"For God so loved the world, that He gave His only begotten Son, that whosoever believeth in Him should not perish, but have everlasting life."

The Power of Love

Love is a small word with a gigantic meaning. We begin with God's love—His example. God loved the world so much that He gave what was most precious to Him—His only Son. Through this act, God set the standard for true love. We love, so we give. Love is not just expressed in words; it is demonstrated through action. Love is an *action word*.

Love is Demonstrative

Love is not a private matter; it is demonstrative. Anyone can *say* they love, but without corresponding action, the word loses its meaning. Love is visible. Love is tangible. Love can be felt and recognized by everyone.

- Love can be learned.
- Love can be shared.
- Love starts in the heart.

Jesus gave us the most important commandment for living a victorious life.

Matthew 22:37-39
"Jesus said unto him, 'Thou shalt love the Lord thy God with all thy heart, and with all thy soul, and with all thy mind. This is the first and great commandment. And the second is like unto it, Thou shalt love thy neighbor as thyself.'"

Jesus tells us to *love our neighbor as we love ourselves.* Love starts with us.

Love Begins Within

Love starts from within. It begins in the heart. We do not have to

search far to find the love of God because Scripture tells us in **Romans 5:5**:
"The love of God is shed abroad in our hearts by the Holy Ghost."

If you feel you do not have *the God kind of love,* all you need to do is ask. All you need to do is give your life to the Lord Jesus Christ, and love will enter. The Holy Spirit will deposit the love of God into your heart. You will receive *the God kind of love,* and it is within your power to exercise that love.

Your life will never be the same. When you exercise the love of God in any measure, it brings powerful results.

The Impact of Love

The love we give:
- Reflects Who God is.
- Describes the One who is greater than we are.
- Gives hope to others.
- Encourages others to cling to life in the face of loss.
- Brings hope to those in despair.
- Strengthens the faint of heart.
- Shines brightly and dispels darkness.
- Heals the sick.
- Inspires others to give and share.
- Makes miracles happen.
- Always revisits our lives.
- Shines through us and blesses us.
- Brings redemption to those around us.
- Changes the world.
- Covers a multitude of sins.
- Kindles in others the desire to embrace life.

PRAYER

Heavenly Father, in the name of Jesus, I thank You for being the personification of love. *You are Love.* I thank You that You taught us to love. I thank You that Your love is shed abroad in our hearts by the Holy Spirit.

I am grateful that the love You place in our hearts, and the love we give, will never leave our lives. Today, I pray that I walk in and exercise the love of God, which is poured into my heart by the Holy Spirit.

I pray that everyone I meet today will experience Your love—not only through my words, not only through my actions, but through my attitude toward others.

Thank You for being the ultimate example of love. May I walk in love as You have demonstrated because Your Word says, Lord Jesus, *"As You are, so are we in this world."*

You gave Your life in love; may I live my life demonstrating that same love with Your help.

In Jesus's name, I pray. Amen.

1 John 4:7-8
"Beloved, let us love one another, for love is of God; and everyone that loveth is born of God, and knoweth God. He that loveth not knoweth not God, for God is love."

MARRIAGE

Genesis 1:26-28
"And God said, Let us make man in our image, after our likeness: and let them have dominion over the fish of the sea, and over the fowl of the air, and over the cattle, and over all the earth, and over every creeping thing that creepeth upon the earth. So God created man in His own image, in the image of God created He him; male and female created He them. And God blessed them, and God said unto them, Be fruitful, and multiply, and replenish the earth, and subdue it: and have dominion over the fish of the sea, and over the fowl of the air, and over every living thing that moveth upon the earth."

The Creation of Man and Woman

God created the heavens and the earth by the power of His Word. But when it came to man, He did not merely speak him into existence. He released His creative power to design and form man from the dust of the earth—meticulously crafting him.

Upon completing His creation, God saw that it was not good for man to be alone. Although Adam was His companion in the cool of the day, enjoying fellowship with the Lord God Almighty, God recognized that Adam needed a suitable companion.

The Creation of Woman

The account continues in **Genesis 2:20-24**:
"And Adam gave names to all cattle, and to the fowl of the air, and to every beast of the field; but for Adam, there was not found a help meet for him. And the LORD God caused a deep sleep to fall upon Adam, and he slept: and He took one of his ribs, and closed up the flesh instead thereof. And the rib, which the LORD God had taken from man, made He a woman, and brought her unto the man. And Adam said, This is now bone of my bones, and flesh of my flesh: she shall be called Woman, because she was taken out of Man. Therefore shall a man leave his father and his mother and shall cleave unto his wife: and they shall be one flesh."

To resolve the issue of loneliness, God created *woman* as a *helpmeet* for

Adam—a completion of His perfect creation.

God's Plan for Marriage

The institution of marriage was part of God's divine plan for humanity—not only for companionship and fellowship but also for procreation. For this reason, He made them male and female.

Marriage is the *first institution* established by God Himself. It is a holy covenant created from the heart of God and placed on the earth for His glory. The union between a man and a woman is *marriage*.

A United Purpose

Not only did God create man and woman for each other, but He also gave them a united plan and purpose to fulfill.

Genesis 1:28 declares:
"And God blessed them, and God said unto them, Be fruitful, and multiply, and replenish the earth, and subdue it: and have dominion over the fish of the sea, and over the fowl of the air, and over every living thing that moveth upon the earth."

God gave them authority over all creation—not only power but also the responsibility to govern and maintain order.

The Significance of Marriage in God's Plan

Since marriage is the *original institution* established by God, it is essential to understand His purpose and plan for that union. Every marriage creates a family unit, and when that family unit fulfills its purpose, it establishes a strong community.

God designed the family with structure and order, commissioning married couples to *leave their father and mother* and *cleave to their spouse*. According to His original design, strong families create strong communities, and His love for the family unit sets the foundation for order in the earth.

PRAYER

Heavenly Father, in the name of Jesus, I thank You for Your original plan for the institution of marriage—bringing one man and one woman together as one flesh, to govern, set order, and fulfill Your divine plan and purpose for families.

I pray that You would rebuild the institution of marriage in this present generation and establish Your boundaries and guidelines so that people may walk in obedience to Your Word.
Help us to walk in obedience to Your original plan—to be fruitful, multiply, replenish the earth, subdue it, and have dominion.

I pray that You will raise up godly marriages to serve as examples to those who may not understand the true meaning and purpose of marriage as You designed it. I pray, in the name of Jesus, that I may return to my first love—my love for You, my love for Your Word, and my love for Your plan and purpose for my life.

I praise and thank You for establishing the institution of marriage between a man and a woman. I give You praise, honor, and glory for Your perfect plan concerning marriage.

In Jesus's name, I pray. Amen.

Proverbs 18:22
"Whoso findeth a wife findeth a good thing, and obtaineth favor of the LORD."

OBEDIENCE

Joshua 22:5
"But take diligent heed to do the commandment and the law, which Moses the servant of the LORD charged you, to love the LORD your God, and to walk in all His ways, and to keep His commandments, and to cleave unto Him, and to serve Him with all your heart and with all your soul."

What is Obedience?

The definition of *obedience*, in simple terms, means knowing the Word of God and acting upon it. It implies aligning our will with God's will—doing what He has asked us to do. Obedience is when we completely surrender to His authority, basing our decisions and actions on His Word. It is the condition or quality of being obedient, characterized by dutiful or submissive behavior.

The Power of Obedience

Obedience is God's pathway to reward our lives.
It establishes order in the home, at work, in the community, in the nation, and in the world. No man is an island unto himself. There is an established order, with commandments and protocols necessary to achieve purpose and destiny.

As our Creator, God has instituted guidance, rules, laws, and commandments for our protection and safety. These laws and principles are vital for the success of mankind and the fulfillment of purpose and destiny. If everyone created their own version of law and order, the world would descend into total chaos, with people moving in countless directions, achieving nothing meaningful.

The Importance of Obedience to God

For this reason, as God's creation, our first commitment in maintaining law and order is obedience to the Word of God. God has attached great promises and benefits to those who walk in obedience to His Word. He knows the *beginning from the end,* and His commandments are designed to lead us into His perfect will.

Our commitment to total obedience to the Word of God, His commandments, and His direction should be absolute.

The Final Authority

Ultimately, the only One to whom we must answer and give an account is God Himself. For this reason, our priorities, our dealings, and our mandates should be first and foremost to keep God's law and walk in obedience.

- *Only then* can we be blessed.
- *Only then* can we achieve and live in victory.
- *Only then* can we walk in total satisfaction, purpose, destiny, and appreciation of life.

Since human vision and insight are limited, our desire to follow and obey God's commandments should be paramount. His way is perfect, and His Word is true.

PRAYER

Heavenly Father, in the name of Jesus, I know that all good things come from You. You have given me Your Word to lead me in the right direction, to walk pleasing in Your sight, to have success in life, and to spend eternity with You.

For this reason, I ask by Your grace that You help me walk in total obedience to Your Word. Your Word is truth that never fails. Your Word gives life its true meaning. Your Word is the light that guides my path.
I pray that, day by day, I will walk in total obedience to Your Word—living a life that is pleasing in Your sight. I thank You for the rewards and blessings that come through obedience to Your Word.

I give You glory, honor, and praise, in Jesus's mighty name.
Amen.

Acts 5:29
"Then Peter and the other apostles answered and said, 'We ought to obey God rather than men.'"

PATIENCE

Psalm 27:14
"Wait on the LORD: be of good courage, and He shall strengthen thine heart: wait, I say, on the LORD."

The Power of Patience

There is a common saying: *"All good things come to those who wait."* However, in our microwave generation, we have adopted a mindset of *instant gratification*. We expect everything to happen instantly. We don't want to wait at the bank, stand in line, wait for a train, or sit in traffic. Impatience has become so prevalent that it sometimes leads to frustration, and even violence. Everyone is searching for immediate results in every area of life.

The Natural Process of Waiting

Nature itself teaches us about the process of *planting and reaping*. There is a time to plant, a time to nurture, and a time to harvest. It takes *patience* to see the fruits of labor. There is no true *instant gratification* in life. Any form of instant gain is often short-lived and unsatisfying.

God gave us the perfect example during the creation of the world. He created the world in six days. For His satisfaction, He focused on one aspect of creation each day, reviewed it, examined it, saw that it was good, and then stopped. He waited until the next day to continue. *Patience.* God demonstrated patience in creation, even though He had the power to do it all in one day. He wants us to do the same—*to exercise patience,* to *adjust our attitude,* and to *wait upon the Lord.*

The Wisdom of Waiting

Because of our human limitations—our lack of foresight and finite understanding—we must stop, think, and reflect before taking action. *Meditation before movement* is key. There are countless blind spots in our future that only God knows. That is why we must *wait on the Lord* to receive guidance and direction from Him.

Even Jesus, despite being Almighty and All-Powerful, calculated His actions. In the Book of John, He said, *"I only say those things I hear the Father say, and I only do those things which the Father does."*

He had a guideline, a plumb line. He had divine direction on what to do and when to do it. He exercised *patience*. This serves as an example for us. We need to calculate our actions, ponder decisions, and take stock of our circumstances before moving forward. Being patient allows us to avoid pitfalls and missteps that we are unaware of.

The Vision Takes Time

Even the Prophet Habakkuk, when he received the vision from the Lord, knew that God's Word would come to pass, but not always immediately.

He wrote in **Habakkuk 2:3**:
"For the vision is yet for an appointed time, but at the end it shall speak, and not lie: though it tarry, wait for it; because it will surely come, it will not tarry."

Though it may take time—*though it tarries*—we are called to *wait*, to *exercise patience*, and not to run ahead. We must lean on God for His perfect timing in every situation. As we do so, He will give us direction, because His Word never fails.

Patience: A Fruit of the Spirit

The *fruit of the Spirit—patience—*gives us the ability to wait. This is the Lord Himself working in our lives, restraining us from rushing ahead, keeping us from problems and issues that we are not equipped to handle. We must *wait upon the Lord*. Our daily motto should be: *Wait upon the Lord. Be patient. Exercise patience.*

PRAYER

Heavenly Father, in the name of Jesus, I give You thanks and praise for providing everything I need for a successful life. I acknowledge You as my Lord and my Savior. You know my end from my beginning; my path is already established and written in Your perfect plan.

In the mighty name of Jesus, I ask that You grant me the grace to *wait upon You,* to not rush ahead but to trust in Your perfect timing. I praise and thank You for the plans and purposes You have for my life.

I pray that I will continue to *wait upon You, Lord God,* with patience, allowing Your will and purposes to be accomplished in my life. May the fruit of *patience* be demonstrated in my life through the Holy Spirit.
In Jesus's name, I pray. Amen.

Hebrews 10:23
"Let us hold fast the profession of our faith without wavering; for He is faithful that promised."

PEACE

Philippians 4:6-7
"Be anxious for nothing, but in everything by prayer and supplication with thanksgiving let your requests be made known to God. And the peace of God, which surpasses all understanding, shall guard your hearts and minds through Christ Jesus."

The Source of True Peace

This passage of Scripture suggests that peace comes from God, but it also requires our cooperation. Peace is, in many ways, a matter of choice. The verse refers to the *"peace of God."* This implies that there are different kinds of peace, leading to an important question: *What kind of peace should we embrace?*

We should also examine ourselves to understand what gives us peace. Where does our peace come from?

Peace is meant to be experienced in both the heart and the mind. Our success and confidence in life reflect the peace we carry within. For lasting peace, we need to examine the source of that peace. The only eternal value in life is what we receive from God and His Word—our true source of peace.

Carefree Through Trust in God

The Scripture reference encourages us to be carefree about everything. We should not stress or worry, but instead, take all our concerns to God in prayer, trusting Him and giving thanks for His answers.

This act of surrender guarantees that *"the peace of God"* will rule and reign in our hearts and minds through Christ Jesus. We will experience His peace, much like the calm in the eye of a storm—resting in it just as Jesus did when He slept through the storm that raged around Him.

Isaiah 26:3
"You will keep him in perfect peace, whose mind is stayed on You, because he trusts in You."

This verse speaks of *perfect peace,* teaching us to look to our Savior and Redeemer as the only true source of spiritual gifts, including peace. This is not the kind of peace that the world gives—it is perfect peace. To experience this perfect peace, we must not simply communicate with, serve, or rest in Christ occasionally. It requires a constant attitude—a life decision to put our faith and trust entirely in God. This guarantees perfect peace even in the midst of life's storms and chaos.

PRAYER

Heavenly Father, thank You for making provision for my well-being. Thank You for the fulfillment of Your Word, which guarantees my peace in You. I cast all my cares upon You, knowing

that You care for me.

I trust that You have already made provision for my welfare, which includes Your peace. Today, I open my heart and receive the peace of God—the perfect peace that comes from keeping my mind consciously focused on who You are.

In the name of Jesus, I choose to live day by day in the peace of God, which surpasses all understanding. Thank You, Father, in Jesus's name. Amen.

Colossians 3:15
"And let the peace of God rule in your hearts, to which also you were called in one body; and be thankful."

PRAYER

John 14:13-14
"And whatever you shall ask in My name, that will I do, that the Father may be glorified in the Son. If you shall ask anything in My name, I will do it."

The Power and Purpose of Prayer

Prayer is the result of a relationship with God. It is an expression of trust in God, acknowledging that He is Almighty and All-powerful, capable of fulfilling all that He has promised in His Word.

Prayer is talking to God—having a conversation with Him. The most important part of any conversation is having your questions answered. An essential aspect of that conversation is knowing you are being heard. If you are not being heard, the conversation becomes meaningless, a waste of time for both you and the other person.

In the context of prayer, it is about having a meaningful conversation with God, whether or not we think the matter is significant.

Approaching God in Prayer

Prayer is approaching God with respect and honor as the Almighty, true, and living God. When we pray, we come before Him as our Creator—the One who gave us life, who sent us to this earth with purpose, a plan, and a destiny to fulfill. God takes every conversation with His children seriously.
For this reason, before approaching God in prayer, we should be properly prepared in our words, our hearts, our attitudes, and our actions. Our attitude and actions should align with the honor and respect due to God, the sovereign Creator of all things.

Growing in Prayer and Relationship

As our relationship with God grows, so does the power of our prayers. As our faith and trust in God increase, His trust in us to bring our desires and requests to reality also grows.

Prayer is also the result of knowing the will of God and working with Him to see it fulfilled on earth. Prayer is the activation process for what God desires to accomplish in the world.

The spirit of prayer and intercession comes upon those whose hearts are open to God's will and purposes. God entrusts these individuals with His plans and purposes, to be accomplished through prayer.

The Honor and Privilege of Prayer

Approaching God in prayer is both a great honor and a privilege. God is not obligated to do anything more for us than what He has already done. Yet, because He is a loving Father, He encourages us to come to Him anytime, in any situation, and under any circumstance.

It is a profound privilege to know that whenever we come to God in prayer, He is attentive to our requests. He hears us, He cares about what concerns us, and He is able to answer and provide results.

1 Thessalonians 5:17
"Pray without ceasing."

Time spent with God is of utmost importance. Our God is a verbal God. He created us to be verbal beings as well. Our conversation with God should be constant. We should never be silent when the Almighty God is attentive to our voice, receptive to our requests, and willing to provide answers.

He has given us the assurance that whatever we ask in His name, He will do it because it brings glory to His Name. Anything we ask, He will provide. No one is excluded from this promise. We should always come to God in prayer—always.

PRAYER

Heavenly Father, I thank You that I can come to You in prayer at any time, knowing that You hear me and will answer my prayers. I thank

You for Your promise that when I call, You will hear and respond. In Jesus's name, I come, and in Jesus's name, I pray. Amen.

Psalm 65:2
"O You who hear prayer, unto You shall all flesh come."

PROMISE

2 Peter 1:4
"Whereby are given unto us exceeding great and precious promises: that by these ye might be partakers of the divine nature, having escaped the corruption that is in the world through lust."

The Power of a Promise

It is often said that a promise is a debt, and a debt must be paid. According to Webster's definition, a *promise* is *"a declaration or assurance that one will do a particular thing or that a particular thing will happen."* It means to assure someone that something will definitely be done, given, or arranged; it is an undertaking or declaration that something will happen. Promises provide good grounds for expecting a particular outcome or situation—all positive declarations.

Trust and Hope in Promises

We can only receive promises from someone we know and trust. A promise is a pledge—something we look forward to. A promise is the hope that our desires, needs, and wants will be fulfilled.

A good promise brings excitement to life. It makes the sun shine brighter and puts a spring in our steps. A good promise brightens our day and fills us with hope for the future.

The Promises of God

Now, let us shift our minds to the promises of God. The referenced Scripture reminds us that God has given us *exceedingly great and precious promises*. God's promises allow us to be partakers of His divine nature.

His promises bring the hope of salvation, assuring us that we can change from a life of sin and hopelessness to a life of victory in Him. His promises encourage us to walk in triumph, to become better people in every area of our lives.

Through His promises, we can walk in divine health and healing; we can have victory over our enemies. He promises to fight our battles and never leave us alone. We can always look forward to bigger and better things in Him.

Building a Relationship with God

For this reason, our lives should be dedicated to building our relationship with God and securing the richness of His promises, allowing them to be manifested in our lives. A strong relationship with Him positions us to receive His promises fully and completely.

PRAYER

Heavenly Father, thank You that Your Word is truth. Your Word will accomplish everything that You have sent it to do. Your Word is Your promise; Your Word is Your truth. The fulfillment of Your promises in my life brings me into the richness of all You have purposed and planned for my destiny on this earth.

As I continue to learn, obey, and grow in my relationship with You, I pray for the future manifestation of Your promises in my life.
In the name of Jesus. Amen.

2 Corinthians 1:20
"For all the promises of God in Him are yes, and in Him, Amen, to the glory of God through us."

PROSPERITY

Joshua 1:8
"This book of the law shall not depart from your mouth, but you shall meditate on it day and night, that you may observe to do according to all that is written in it. For then you will make your way prosperous, and then you will have good success."

The Origin of Prosperity

Prosperity begins and ends with God. It is God's plan to provide for His children. God allows prosperity to enter our lives as we apply ourselves to the truth of His Word, allowing it to become part of our everyday living.

There is no lack or insufficiency in God. The Scriptures declare in **Psalm 23:1**:
"The Lord is my shepherd; I shall not want."

Because the Lord is in charge of my life—because I have given Him rule and reign over my life—I have no need. This means I have no need spiritually, emotionally, physically, or materially. God, in all His sufficiency, enriches my life because of my relationship with Him.

God's Ownership and Provision

As our Heavenly Father, who owns everything and created the entire world, there is nothing outside of His command or authority. Because He is all-sufficient, He has extended His gracious provision of prosperity to His children.

Every loving father, every parent, and even those who may not fully understand love still provide for their children according to their means. How much more, then, will our Heavenly Father, who owns everything, provide for us?

The Nature of True Prosperity

True prosperity brings with it an internal peace and satisfaction that encompasses the whole being. There is a synchronization of the spirit, soul, and body when true prosperity is present in our lives. As we walk according to God's Word, we experience no need or lack.

We are guaranteed prosperity and good success in everything we do when we follow His principles. His promises are sure, and His provision is always more than enough.

PRAYER

Heavenly Father, in the name of Jesus, I give You praise and thanks for the prosperity You have provided for my whole being—spirit, soul, and body. Your provision brings peace and tranquility into my life. You supply all my needs according to Your riches in glory, for You are the Great Creator.

I look to You for every aspect of provision in my life. Thank You for providing more than enough so that those who are close to me can also experience Your abundance and prosperity. I give You thanks and praise, knowing that every good gift comes from You. There is success, victory, and prosperity in my life because I seek You first, and all things are added to me.

I give You thanks and praise for all these things, in Jesus's wonderful name. Amen.

Luke 6:38
"Give, and it shall be given unto you; good measure, pressed down, shaken together, and running over, shall men give into your bosom. For with the same measure that you use, it shall be measured to you again."

PROTECTION

Psalm 91:14-15
"Because he has set his love upon Me, therefore I will deliver him; I will set him on high because he has known My name. He shall call upon Me, and I will answer him; I will be with him in trouble; I will deliver him and honor him."

God's Sovereign Protection

In His sovereign wisdom, God has established contingency plans of protection for His creation.

Our security and protection are covered by the blood of Jesus. Just as God instructed Moses to apply the blood of a lamb to the doorposts of the Israelites' homes so that when the death angel passed, everyone inside would be protected, God has also established protection for us through the blood of Jesus.

We do not need to fear or be afraid as long as we walk according to God's will and purposes for our lives. His protection is secure and unwavering.

The Ministry of Angels

God has also established protection for His creation through the ministry of angels. Angels are ministering spirits sent to serve those who are heirs of salvation. We, as children of God, are heirs of salvation—purchased by Jesus through His redemptive work.

The angels of God have been assigned to protect us as we go in and as we go out. Nothing and no one can withstand or overcome the power of God's angels—mighty creatures created by God for our safety.

Protection Through the Word of God

Our protection is further secured by the Word of God. When we apply His Word to our lives and walk in obedience, the Word becomes our shield. The Word of God is His truth, His life, and His testimony.

Everything that comes from God is good, powerful, and mighty. Therefore, when we align ourselves with His Word in obedience, we are protected by His promises.

The Scriptures assure us in **Jude 1:24**:
"Now unto Him that is able to keep you from falling, and to present you faultless before the presence of His glory with exceeding joy."

God is able to keep us from falling; our protection is secure. He promises to protect us to the very end. We are safe under His watchful care.

Protection in All Places and Times

As we move about in our daily lives, going in and coming out, we cannot fully account for the many times God has extended His protection toward us. Whether traveling by land, sea, or air, God's protection is secure, no matter where we are.

Just as God is omnipresent, His protection over His children is also ever-present. He is always with us, ensuring our safety.

PRAYER

Heavenly Father, in the name of Jesus, I give You praise, honor, and glory for Your divine protection over my life. You watch over my going out and my coming in, and You know all my movements.

I am secure, knowing that You have already given Your angels charge over me. I thank You for Your Word of safety and protection, which will accomplish everything You have declared.

Thank You for protecting me day and night. You guard me even when I am unaware of the dangers around me. Thank You for releasing me into the care of Your angels. Thank You for guiding my footsteps.

Thank You for covering me with the blood of Jesus and the Word of life. Thank You for surrounding me on every side, day and night. I confidently declare and rest assured in Your protection.

Father, I give You glory, honor, and praise in the mighty name of Jesus. Amen.

Jude 1:24-25
"Now unto Him who is able to keep you from falling, and to present you faultless before the presence of His glory with exceeding joy, to the only wise God our Savior, be glory and majesty, dominion and power, both now and forever. Amen."

PURPOSE

1 John 3:8
"For this purpose the Son of God was manifested, that He might destroy the works of the devil."

The Question of Purpose

Many people have never truly faced the question: *Why am I here?* It may not seem like a deep question, but it is a significant one. *Why am I here? Why am I alive? Why was I sent into the world? Is there a reason I am here, and what am I supposed to do with this life?*

The Scriptures clearly reveal the purpose of Jesus's coming into the world. Jesus came *"to destroy the works of the devil."* He came to eliminate sin and show us the way out. He came to give us everlasting life—eternal life with Him and the Father in heaven. Jesus came to heal us of all sicknesses and diseases. He gave His life so that our sins could be washed away, making us clean, without guilt or blame. Jesus came to destroy everything that is evil.

Why Am I Here?

Now, back to the question: *Why am I here?*

- What am I doing with my life right now?
- What have I done with my life so far?
- What do I plan to do in the future?
- What are my goals and my plans?

Do these goals align with God's perfect will for me? Am I contributing anything meaningful to society? When I leave this world, will anyone remember who I was? Will anyone remember my contributions? Will anyone remember that I was even here?

It has been said that cemeteries are full of gifts and talents that people never used or contributed to society. Will that be said of you? *What is your contribution?*

A Time for Introspection

This is a moment for introspection:

- *Why am I here?*
- *What is my purpose for being here?*
- *What is my purpose for living?*
- *What is my purpose for being born?*

While we are alive, we must effectively pursue and accomplish our purpose on earth. God sent each one of us into this world with a plan and a purpose. Our first goal should be to seek out God's plan and purpose for our lives. We need to recognize our gifts and talents and invest them in the Kingdom of God for true fulfillment.

Discovering Your Purpose

Let today be the beginning of a new chapter in your life.

- Spend time reflecting on your purpose.
- Speak to yourself; ask the deep questions.
- Discover the reason you are here.

Ask yourself: *What is my contribution to society? How am I affecting my family, my church, and my community? Will anyone remember me and my deeds after I am gone?*
Can you confidently say, *Yes, I am walking in purpose. I am fulfilling my divine goals in life*?

PRAYER

Heavenly Father, in the name of Jesus, I come to You. I pray that You reveal Your plan and purpose for my life. I ask for understanding of what You have sent me into this world to accomplish.

By Your grace and with Your anointing, I submit myself to obey and fulfill Your plan and purpose for my life. I give You thanks and praise for clarifying my assignment and granting me understanding of what, when, and where.

In Jesus's mighty name. Amen.

Romans 8:28
"And we know that all things work together for good to them that love God, to them who are the called according to His purpose."

RIGHTEOUSNESS

Isaiah 54:17
"No weapon formed against you shall prosper, and every tongue that rises against you in judgment you shall condemn. This is the heritage of the servants of the Lord, and their righteousness is from Me," says the Lord.

The Righteousness of God in Christ

Jesus teaches that we are the righteousness of God in Him. There is no righteousness found in man on his own. When God looks at His children—those who have accepted Jesus as their Lord and Savior—He sees us clothed in the robe of righteousness.

We have taken on the attributes of Jesus. We are in right standing with God. He sees us just as He sees Jesus. It is important for us to understand that, in ourselves, there is no righteousness. Humanity fell away from God and His ways, but by receiving Jesus Christ as our Lord and Savior, we have been dressed in a robe of righteousness. God now recognizes us as He does Jesus.

Growing in Righteousness

We are not yet perfected, as humanity had strayed from God's ways. However, as our relationship with Him grows, we walk in and become the righteousness of God in Christ Jesus.

The Word of God teaches us that our righteousness is of God—not because of anything we have done or who we are. Our righteousness is solely because we accepted the Lord Jesus, we walk in His ways, and we are obedient to His Word.

What Righteousness Means

Righteousness also means that we are in good standing with God, that we are in a relationship with Him. As we continue to exercise our faith and walk in righteousness, we can be confident that God will sustain us and equip us with everything we need to remain strong in Him.

We are His, and He sees us through the lens of His Son, Jesus Christ. Our standing with God is secure, not because of our works, but because of His grace.

PRAYER

Father, in the name of Jesus, I thank You that I am the righteousness of God in Him. It is not because of anything I have done but because of who Jesus is. Receiving Jesus as my Lord and Savior has granted me righteousness in Him.

I thank You that You receive me just as You receive Jesus. I am grateful that day by day, You are working out Your righteousness in me. I am becoming stronger and more purposeful in Your ways.

Thank You for clothing me with the robe of righteousness. Thank You for seeing me the way You see Jesus. I give You glory, honor, and praise in Jesus's matchless name. Amen.

Philippians 3:9
"And be found in Him, not having my own righteousness, which is from the law, but that which is through faith in Christ—the righteousness which is of God by faith."

SALVATION

John 3:16
"For God so loved the world that He gave His only begotten Son, that whoever believes in Him should not perish but have everlasting life."

The Gift of Salvation

Salvation means to be saved, to be rescued. Humanity needed to be saved and rescued—but rescued from whom and rescued from what? We were alienated and separated from God, who created us in His image to have daily fellowship with Him.

God's original design was for us to have an unbroken relationship with Him—no barriers, no hindrances. However, sin entered the world when man disobeyed God, causing separation from His presence.

God's Original Plan and the Fall of Man

In God's original plan, He intended for humanity to have fellowship with Him and Him alone. He designed man for eternal happiness and communion with Him. However, man's disobedience led to the fall, breaking the fellowship and disrupting God's intended plan.

The Plan of Salvation

The plan of salvation was conceived between God the Father and Jesus Christ. Scripture teaches that God sent a Savior, a Redeemer, who came to *"seek and save that which was lost."* Humanity was lost and in need of redemption.

In His great love and mercy, God chose to send His only begotten Son, the Lord Jesus Christ, as the sacrificial Lamb to redeem mankind. God required a spotless, unblemished sacrifice to restore humanity to its original place. Jesus Christ became that sacrifice, giving His life in exchange for ours.

We needed a Savior, and we found the answer in **Luke 19:10**:
"For the Son of Man has come to seek and to save that which was lost."
The Universality of Salvation

Salvation is available to anyone who recognizes they are lost and in need of a Savior. Jesus Christ is that Savior. He died on the cross and gave His life so that we might have life. Jesus took our place on the cross and died for our sins—not His own, for He was spotless and without sin. He took our place to bring us salvation.

Through His sacrifice and our acceptance of Jesus as our Savior, we pass from death to life. We are saved. We have salvation. Old things are passed away, and behold, all things have become new. We are new creations in Christ. We are saved, delivered, and set free, restored to fellowship with God the Father as He originally intended.

2 Corinthians 5:17 reminds us:
"Therefore, if anyone is in Christ, he is a new creature: old things are passed away; behold, all things have become new."

PRAYER

Heavenly Father, I give You thanks and praise for Your perfect plan of salvation.

Jesus, thank You for fulfilling the plan of redemption and restoring fellowship with God, my Father.

Thank You for taking upon Yourself all my sin, my sicknesses, and my diseases, purchasing my redemption. Because of You, today I am saved, healed, and delivered. You took my place and paid a debt You did not owe.
Now I walk in divine health and healing, and I have restored fellowship with God. I thank You for being the ultimate sacrifice, saving mankind from the burden of sin caused by man's disobedience. Thank You for the total plan of salvation, accomplished through the shedding of Your precious blood.

All glory, honor, and praise belong to You, Almighty Father, in Jesus's name. Amen.

Romans 10:9-10
"That if you confess with your mouth the Lord Jesus and believe in your heart that God has raised Him from the dead, you will be saved. For with the heart one believes unto righteousness, and with the mouth, confession is made unto salvation."

THANKSGIVING

Psalm 100:4
"Enter into His gates with thanksgiving, and into His courts with praise: be thankful unto Him, and bless His name."

The Importance of Thanksgiving

The Holy Scriptures admonish us over one hundred times to give thanks to God, to express thanksgiving to Him—not to any other person, but to God Almighty. Even as we approach God, His Word has provided us with the proper protocol to enter into His presence.

Just as there is protocol for entering the presence of earthly dignitaries—security checks and levels of clearance—God's protocol for entering His presence is clearly stated: *"Enter His gates with thanksgiving."*

An Attitude of the Heart

Thanksgiving is an attitude of the heart. If you are not thankful, it means you are not experiencing gratification or success in certain areas of your life. When we examine ourselves and our situations, and compare them with what is happening around us—in our communities, in the nation, and in the world—there is so much for which we should be thankful.

We may not have everything we think we need, but there is always someone with less, someone in a more dire situation than ourselves.

Reasons to Be Thankful

Think of this:

- Thousands, even hundreds of thousands, of people—adults and children—went to bed hungry last night without food.
- Many homeless individuals slept on the streets, exposed to the elements, without shelter or a roof over their heads.

- Countless people are currently lying in hospital beds, suffering under the weight of sickness and disease.
- Some are experiencing loneliness because their family and friends have abandoned them.

When we compare where we are to these situations, what is our response? Do we take our own situation for granted, thinking that our lives could never change like those around us?

A Heart of Gratitude

Our hearts should overflow with thanksgiving to God for who He is and what He has done in our lives. This attitude of gratitude should not be limited to a moment; it should be an all-day occurrence.

We are called to be thankful not only for the spiritual blessings—such as salvation and reconciliation with God—but also for the tangible gifts: protection, provision, and the life He has allowed us to enjoy.

Thankfulness in the Small Things

We must be thankful for the simple things in life:

- Thankful that we can see.
- Thankful that we can walk.
- Thankful for two arms and two legs.
- Thankful for loved ones.
- Thankful for friends.
- Thankful for our employers and employees.

Thankful. Thankful. Thankful.

There is so much to be grateful for if we just stop for a moment and consider where we are at this point in time—reflecting on where we were 10 years ago, 20 years ago.

Let us testify of the goodness of God and be grateful for all He has done in our lives.

PRAYER

Heavenly Father, in the name of Jesus, my heart is overwhelmed with thanksgiving and gratitude to You for who You are. Thank You for keeping me in Your thoughts and planning out a life that I can enjoy.

Thank You for family and friends. Thank You for protection and for providing abundantly for Your children. Thank You for life today, in a world where circumstances and situations are constantly changing.

Thank You, Father, for always being mindful of me. Words are not adequate to express all the thanks and gratitude You deserve.
In Jesus's name, I thank You. Amen.

Philippians 4:6
"Be anxious for nothing; but in everything, by prayer and supplication with thanksgiving, let your requests be made known unto God."

THE FEAR OF THE LORD

Psalm 115:12-13
"The Lord has been mindful of us; He will bless us; He will bless the house of Israel; He will bless the house of Aaron. He will bless those who fear the Lord, both small and great."

Recognizing God's Greatness

We must recognize and acknowledge God for who He is—the Great Almighty God. Acknowledging that He is all-powerful and all-knowing—*El Shaddai, the Great I Am*—should instill a reverential fear of the Lord in our hearts.

Understanding that the one true and living God loves us deeply, desires to fellowship with us, and longs to bless us, should leave us speechless and in awe. Believing that all His great and mighty promises are ours should cause us to humble ourselves before Him—just as subjects bow before earthly kings and queens.

What is "The Fear of the Lord"?

The Fear of the Lord refers to a profound sense of respect, awe, and submission to the Lord. We walk in the fear of the Lord not out of terror or fright, but out of deep honor, respect, and adoration for who He is.

We cannot truly know God in His fullness until we possess reverential appreciation, respect, and admiration for Him, taking Him seriously and honoring His Word.

Approaching God with Proper Perspective

When approaching God, we must keep our minds in proper perspective. His will and His plan for our lives lead us into destiny and are always far above our own plans.

When we walk in obedience, God sees that we honor Him, acknowledging that He knows what is best for us. God can trust us when we have a reverential fear of Him. We are called to love what He loves, hate what He hates, and prioritize what is important to Him. We cannot be casual about our walk with God. *The fear of the Lord is to hate evil.*

Proverbs 9:10 teaches:
"The fear of the Lord is the beginning of wisdom, and the knowledge of the Holy One is understanding."

The fear of the Lord embraces wisdom. We need wisdom to live a successful life, and when we have *The Fear of the Lord,* we walk in wisdom.

Honoring Those We Respect

In everyday life, there are people we respect and honor.

- How do you treat someone you deeply admire?
- How do you behave around a king, a queen, a president, or a teacher who has impacted your life?

When you respect someone, you give them your undivided attention. You honor their presence, listen intently to their words, and follow their instructions.

But think about this:

- Do you trust what they say?
- Can they read your mind?
- Can they give you your next breath?
- How accessible are they to you and you alone?

How do you treat the person who signs your paycheck? Do you follow instructions at work? As a teacher, do you follow the curriculum? As a student, do you study and turn in your homework?

Have you ever asked yourself why you do these things without question? Is it because you understand the consequences of not doing them? Would you call that fear, or is it respect?

Comparing Earthly Respect to Godly Fear

When we compare these situations to our relationship with God, do we give Him the honor, respect, and reverence He deserves? He deserves all that and much more.

Hebrews 12:28-29
"Therefore, since we are receiving a kingdom which cannot be shaken, let us have grace, by which we may serve God acceptably with reverence and godly fear. For our God is a consuming fire."

PRAYER

Heavenly Father, I pray that the Spirit of the Fear of the Lord will come upon me so that I may walk worthy and respectfully before You. Help me to honor and obey You in all that You have spoken to my heart.

May the reverential *Fear of the Lord* continually motivate me to walk in obedience so that I may experience Your abundant life. I honor and deeply respect You as the One True and Living God, who holds all things by the word of Your power.

Thank You for Your love and mercy.
In Jesus's name. Amen.

Ecclesiastes 12:13
"Let us hear the conclusion of the whole matter: Fear God and keep His commandments, for this is the whole duty of man."

THE JOY OF THE LORD

Nehemiah 8:10
Then he said unto them, Go your way, eat the fat, and drink the sweet, and send portions unto them for whom nothing is prepared: for this day is holy unto our Lord: neither be ye sorry; for the joy of the Lord is your strength.

Who would have thought that this morning, just one hour after I received the news of a friend passing away overnight, I would be writing about *"The Joy of the Lord."* After the intercessors in the church had been praying for him for the past couple of months—a man of faith, an intercessor himself—who would have thought that after receiving this overwhelming and heartbreaking news, and being deeply moved, I would be singing:

> **Holy is Your Name, Jesus**
> **You deserve the praise**
> **Holy is Your name**
> **Worthy is Your name, Jesus**
> **You deserve the praise**
> **Worthy is Your name**

("Holy is Your Name, Jesus" (Elevation Worship 2018))

Unimaginable, that I would be experiencing such a feeling, which I can only describe as *"The Joy of the Lord."* Out of my heart came this song, glorifying God for who He is.

I went out for a walk to clear my head, and I could not stop singing that song—just an hour after receiving that news. I was feeling and experiencing the loss, and yet the song of the Lord had risen out of my heart, which I can only explain as *"The Joy of the Lord."*

You see, *joy* is a fruit of the Spirit listed in **Galatians 5:22-23**:
"But the fruit of the Spirit is love, joy, peace, longsuffering, gentleness, goodness, faith, meekness, temperance: against such, there is no law."

Joy is the working of the Holy Spirit inside our hearts despite what is happening on the outside, in the natural. Joy works and is manifested even contrary to what we see with our eyes, hear with our ears, or touch with our hands.
Words cannot fully express or explain the workings of the Holy Spirit. We need to be aware of the difference between *"The Joy of the Lord"* and happiness.

According to Webster, joy is *"a feeling of great pleasure and happiness. A source or cause of delight."*

Happiness, according to Webster, is *"the state of being happy."* Other words that describe happiness include contentment, pleasure, and exhilaration.

As children of God, we look to the Word of God for understanding and meaning in the things that affect us. Joy comes from having a relationship with God and keeping His commandments, as Jesus promised in **John 15:10-11**:
"If ye keep My commandments, ye shall abide in My love; even as I have kept My Father's commandments and abide in His love. These things have I spoken unto you, that My joy might remain in you, and that your joy might be full."

You can experience *"The Joy of the Lord"* over every negative situation in your life. *"The Joy of the Lord"* is what comes out of you when everything else around you fails. Happiness is dictated or fueled by outside circumstances. As Christians, we need to walk according to and in tune with the Holy Spirit, who is the only One who can release *"The Joy of the Lord"* in our lives.

Today, I encourage you to allow God to work in your heart and release His joy in you, which will undoubtedly affect everything around you and influence everyone around you in a good and positive way. *"The Joy of the Lord"* is released as you give God control of your life.

PRAYER

Father, in the name of Jesus, I thank You for making provision for every situation in my life. Even in my times of disappointment, grief, and loss, I can experience *the joy of the Lord*. The joy of the Lord, which You said is my strength. Thank You that *the joy of the Lord* overshadows every negative and difficult situation in my life and influences those around me. I ask You right now to release the power of the Holy Spirit in my heart and in my life so that Your joy will overcome any negative or evil work in me. Strengthen me with Your joy today, I ask, in Jesus' Holy Name.

Habakkuk 3:18
"Yet I will rejoice in the Lord, I will joy in the God of my salvation."

THE PERSON OF THE HOLY SPIRIT

1 Corinthians 2:9-10
"But as it is written: 'Eye has not seen, nor ear heard, neither have entered into the heart of man, the things which God has prepared for those who love Him.' But God has revealed them to us by His Spirit, for the Spirit searches all things, yes, the deep things of God."

The Godhead: Three in One

The Godhead is three in one—three distinct persons, yet one God. These are three individual persons with different functions, yet they are one unified essence:

- **God the Father**, who is the Creator and Father of all.
- **Jesus, God the Son**, whose purpose was to fulfill the plan of salvation and who now sits at the right hand of God, continually making intercession for us.
- **God the Holy Spirit**, the Comforter, Teacher, Advocate, and Counselor, whom Jesus left on earth for us when He ascended to heaven.

The Manifestation of the Godhead

The manifestation of the Godhead was beautifully demonstrated during the baptism of Jesus in the Jordan River by John the Baptist.

- The **Father spoke**, and His voice was heard: *"This is My beloved Son, in whom I am well pleased."*
- **Jesus, the Son of God**, was physically baptized in the Jordan.
- **The Holy Spirit** descended upon Jesus in the form of a dove.

The biblical account is found in **Luke 3:22**:
"And the Holy Ghost descended in a bodily shape like a dove upon Him (Jesus), and a voice came from heaven (God the Father), which said, 'You are My beloved Son; in You, I am well pleased.'"

The Person of the Holy Spirit

The Holy Spirit is very real and personal.

- The Holy Spirit **speaks**.
- The Holy Spirit **is grieved**.
- The Holy Spirit **teaches**.
- The Holy Spirit **helps**.
- The Holy Spirit **counsels**.

He possesses attributes of a person and displays true personality traits. Sometimes, in Scripture, He is referred to as the *Holy Ghost*, but He is not a ghost. He is a very real person with personality and emotion.

The Analogy of the Holy Spirit

We can understand the Holy Spirit through the analogy of **water**, which can exist in three different forms:

- Water as **ice**
- Water as **steam**
- Water as **liquid**

The substance is always "water," but its form and function differ. Similarly, the Holy Spirit is part of the Godhead with unique roles and expressions.

Addressing the Holy Spirit Properly

When we speak about the Holy Spirit, we must be conscious to address Him as a **Person**, not as a thing or an "it."

The Holy Spirit, as God, is **Spirit** (capital "S"), which is distinct from the human spirit, represented with a lowercase "s."

The Triune God

Just as a person is made up of **spirit, soul, and body**, so is God represented in three persons:

- **Father**
- **Son**
- **Holy Spirit**

These three are collectively called the **Triune God**. Our reference and interaction with the Holy Spirit should always be from a **person-to-person perspective**.

The Indwelling Presence of the Holy Spirit

When we receive Jesus Christ as Lord and Savior, we ask Him to come into our hearts. This invitation brings the **indwelling presence of the Holy Spirit**, who comes into our hearts and dwells there. Jesus comes in the form of His Spirit, not in a physical form.

PRAYER

Heavenly Father, I thank You for the person of the Holy Spirit. I thank You that by confessing the Lord Jesus and receiving Him into my heart, the Holy Spirit has entered and become one with my spirit. I give You thanks for the indwelling presence of the Holy Spirit.

As the Spirit is one with my spirit, I receive sustaining power by the same Spirit that raised Jesus from the dead. I pray that I will be sensitive to the voice of the Holy Spirit when He leads and guides me into all truth.

I thank You, Father, that You did not leave us alone on this earth, but the Holy Spirit will remain and abide with us while we are here. May I continually be sensitive to the voice of the Holy Spirit and walk in obedience to His direction and counsel.

I give You thanks and praise for the liberty and freedom of the Holy Spirit working in my life.

In Jesus' name. Amen.

John 14:16-17
"And I will pray the Father, and He shall give you another Comforter, that He may abide with you forever; even the Spirit of Truth, whom the world cannot receive, because it sees Him not, neither knows Him. But you know Him; for He dwells with you and shall be in you."

TRUST

Proverbs 3:5-6
"Trust in the Lord with all your heart; and lean not on your own understanding. In all your ways acknowledge Him, and He shall direct your paths."

Trust in the Lord

Trust is a common word with a wide range of applications. According to Webster's Dictionary, trust is defined as *"Firm belief in the reliability, truth, ability, or strength of someone or something. Assured reliance on the character, ability, strength, or truth of someone or something. One in which confidence is placed."*

Our trust can be placed in someone or something.

- You can trust the chair you sit on to hold you without collapsing.
- You can trust the car you drive to take you from one place to another.
- You can trust someone who speaks kind words about you.
- A child trusts you when you throw them into the air, confident that you will catch them and not let them fall.

Levels of Trust

There is a deeper level of trust that involves placing yourself and everything you do in the care of someone else—total trust. Who in our lives truly deserves that kind of trust? When we consider our relationships, we realize we are dealing with imperfect human beings, just like ourselves.

On a higher level, we should place our trust in the Lord with all our hearts, minds, and strength—total trust. We are to abandon ourselves to trusting God completely. He is the only One who deserves and is worthy of our complete trust.

God has given us life. He has provided for us, redeemed us—not just today, but from the very beginning when man first disobeyed Him and failed to trust Him. Even then, He immediately made a plan to reconcile humanity to Himself.

Trust Built on Relationship

Our trust in God is built upon our relationship with Him and the time we spend nurturing that relationship. It comes from knowing who God is, what He has done, and what He can do. Building trust in God means knowing and obeying His Word. It means believing that what He said, He will do.

There is no lie that can be found in God. Not one word of God is untrue. Over time, what God has declared continues to unfold and come to pass. That is true trust. We are to place our full trust in God and His Word, putting all our thoughts and ideas in second place.

Reflective Questions

- Do you trust the One who made the heavens and the earth with your life?
- Do you trust that He will take care of you and provide for you?
- Can you release all the difficult situations in your life into His hands, knowing that He is more than capable of solving them?

PRAYER

Heavenly Father, in the name of Jesus, I come to You with total trust and confidence. You are the One who created the heavens and the earth. You have made mankind in Your image and likeness. You are the Creator of the entire universe.

I put my total trust and confidence in You, entrusting You with my life and believing that You will carry out everything You have purposed in Your heart concerning me. I depend upon You; I rely on You, knowing that Your ways are higher than my ways and Your thoughts are higher than my thoughts.

Because You know the end from the beginning, my trust is completely in You and what You can and will do in and through me. I surrender and trust in Your perfect will and purpose for my life.

I give You thanks and praise, in Jesus' wonderful, holy name. Amen.

Psalm 9:10
"And they that know Your name will put their trust in You; for You, Lord, have not forsaken those who seek You."

TRUTH

John 14:6
"Jesus said to him, 'I am the way, the truth, and the life. No one comes to the Father except through Me.'"

The Unchanging Nature of Truth

Truth is a statement that cannot be changed or altered. Truth is constant. Who and what do we associate with truth? What can we say never changes? Truth was the same in the past, it is the same today, and it will remain the same in the future. Whether we accept it or not, truth remains constant.

God is Truth

God is truth. He existed in the beginning, and He is the same yesterday, today, and forever. There is no change in God. He remains constant and unchanging.

Jesus said, *"I am the way, the truth, and the life."* He is the only way, the truth that never changes.

In **John 16:13**, Jesus said,
"However, when He, the Spirit of truth, has come, He will guide you into all truth; for He shall not speak of Himself, but whatever He hears, that He will speak; and He will show you things to come."

Jesus was speaking of the Holy Spirit, who was to come after He returned to heaven—the Spirit of Truth. Truth is a spirit. Spirits were created by God, and they do not change.

The Stability of God's Truth

When situations around us change, certain elements and aspects of their true meaning may also change. For this reason, the only truth we can rely on and be certain of is **God's truth**. God's truth is His

Word. What He has spoken out of His mouth is unchangeable, and nothing and no one can alter its outcome or meaning.

Examining Our Lives for Truth

We need to examine our lives and determine what is true. What is constant and never changes? Life is filled with continuous changes—changes in our environment, changes in our thought patterns, changes in our habits, and changes in our physical and mental state.

What can we rely on and depend upon in life that does not change and remains true in every situation and circumstance? We can only measure truth by God and faith in His Word, which is the true source of all truth.

Reality vs. Truth

It is often said that our reality is our truth. But in life, our reality changes with every season. It is never constant. As situations change, our "truth" changes.

We must make our reality and our truth dependent on **God's unchanging truth**. We can never fail if we make this decision. His truth is the solid foundation upon which we can stand, regardless of what changes around us.

PRAYER

Heavenly Father, thank You for Your truth. Your Word is truth, and it always brings about what You have declared. May Your truth be the foundation of my life and my world. May my circumstances and situations be governed and ruled by Your truth—truth that is always victorious and unchanging.

In the name of Jesus, I make the decision to walk in Your truth, to live in Your truth, and to speak Your truth.

Amen.

John 8:32
"And you shall know the truth, and the truth shall make you free."

UNDERSTANDING

Psalm 119:130
"The entrance of Your words gives light; it gives understanding to the simple."

Understanding is Knowing

Understanding is knowing. Without understanding, we are walking in the dark, unaware of who we are or what is happening around us. Understanding is the entrance of light into the heart and soul, giving clear direction of who we are and revealing our lack of knowledge about the things around us.

There is no successful or positive experience in life without understanding. Understanding is knowing how to and what is. Understanding is the opposite of ignorance. Walking in ignorance causes our lives to be filled with confusion and chaos. Walking in understanding brings order to our lives and provides clear direction, leaving no doubt about any situation.

The Power of Understanding

Many live in uncertainty with unresolved problems because they lack understanding of the situation. Understanding brings clarity, direction, and truth to our lives. A lack of understanding leaves us in total chaos and turmoil.

True understanding and purpose in life come from the Word of God. **Jeremiah 33:3** records:
"Call unto Me, and I will answer you, and show you great and mighty things, which you do not know."

This passage of Scripture tells us that if we call upon God, we will receive understanding and knowledge of the things we do not know.

Understanding is Spiritual

Imparting understanding is the work of the Holy Spirit in our lives. Understanding is spiritual; it is not physical. We cannot touch or see understanding, but we can clearly identify when we have it. Understanding in our lives provides a great level of knowledge and insight.

PRAYER

Heavenly Father, in the name of Jesus, I pray today that the spirit of understanding fills my heart and my life. Take away all uncertainty and all doubts as I live and move about today. I receive Your Word and lean on You for understanding in the things that concern me.

Thank You for giving me an abundance of understanding to enable me to live a successful life in You and in Your perfect will and direction for my life. In Jesus' name, I ask. Amen.

Proverbs 3:3-4
"Let not mercy and truth forsake you: bind them around your neck; write them upon the table of your heart: So you shall find favor and good understanding in the sight of God and man."

UNITY

Psalm 133:1,3
"Behold, how good and how pleasant it is for brethren to dwell together in unity! ... For there the Lord commanded the blessing, even life forevermore."

The Power of Unity

There is a common saying: *"United we stand, divided we fall."* It is a very practical and easily understood principle. This is similar in meaning to *"One can put a thousand to flight, and two can put ten thousand to flight."* It is practical and easy to understand: one person standing alone is not able to withstand a group.

Unity is one of God's principles according to His Word. When we dwell together in unity, God commands the blessing. God's principle of unity is also reflected in His relationship with the Lord Jesus Christ and the Holy Spirit—the three personalities functioning as one:

- **God the Father**
- **God the Son**
- **God the Holy Spirit**

In His great wisdom and sovereign power, God, not wanting to be alone, created man in His image and likeness. He created a person with whom He could fellowship, speak to, and spend time. It is the perfect example of strength in numbers.

Unity Brings Power

Unity is power. Unity is strength. Unity spells victory and success in every sense of the word. This is demonstrated in the story of the people of Babel, who planned to build a tower that would reach the heavens. The Bible teaches that God Himself came down to investigate their great progress, which He identified as unity and agreement. In order to stop them from achieving their objective, God confused their language, causing them not to understand each other. This created division, and they could no longer work in unity to achieve their goals.

Unity in Our Lives

In our homes and communities, our success is dependent on unity, agreement, togetherness, and love. This principle of unity is such a powerful force that nothing can prevent or hinder people of one heart and one mind from achieving their goals.

Our goal in life for success and victory should be to walk in unity with God, our Creator.

- He has the plans.
- He has the experience.
- He has the ability.

Let us purpose in our minds to be in unity with God. He will lead us on the right path. He will give us the right direction. He will support and strengthen us as we walk in unity with Him. Nothing will be denied or withheld from us when we are in unity with God.

PRAYER

Heavenly Father, I come to You today in the name of Jesus. I pull down everything in my life that would hinder me from walking in unity and love: every wrong thought, selfishness, and self-centeredness. I pray and purpose in my heart today that I will walk in unity and agreement with my brothers and sisters.

Your Word declares that You command the blessing when we live together in unity, when we are together in peace, humbling ourselves to one another. I pray that the spirit of unity will govern my heart, my motives, my will, and every activity.

Thank You for the commanded blessing as I walk and work in unity with those around me, serving You with purpose and destiny.

In Jesus' mighty name, I pray. Amen.

Philippians 2:2-5
"Fulfill my joy by being likeminded, having the same love, being of one accord, of one mind. Let nothing be done through strife or vainglory, but in lowliness of mind let each esteem others better than themselves. Look not every man on his own things, but every man also on the things of others. Let this mind be in you, which was also in Christ Jesus.

VICTORY

1 Corinthians 15:57
"But thanks be to God, who gives us the victory through our Lord Jesus Christ."

The Meaning of Victory

Victory is a condition that every individual would welcome into their lives. Victory means winning. It means achieving. It is success. There are principles involved in gaining victory. Victory assesses your situation with the resources at hand and allows you to make the right, quality decisions. Victory goes hand in hand with wisdom. Wisdom is foreknowing—foretelling in advance the pitfalls and challenges ahead.

Learning from Others

Victory also involves learning from others—imitating those who have gone before us, learning from their mistakes, their challenges, and their achievements. We do not have to make the same mistakes that others made to experience victory. Victory is about calculating our strengths and weaknesses and weighing them against our goals.

Walking in God's Principles

Our main focus for victory is to follow the Word of God, which has all the answers to our questions. Walking with the Lord and serving God according to His principles—godly principles—enables us to walk in victory.

For the battles we are unable to fight, we know that God has us covered. For the challenges that confront us, we know that God will give us the victory. In areas where we are inexperienced, God will provide the support of the Holy Spirit, who is our teacher. There is not one area of our lives where we cannot walk victoriously.

Victory Through Christ Jesus

Through Christ Jesus, God has already made provision for victory in spirit, soul, and body.

- We can have victory in our **soul** by applying the Word of God, changing our thought patterns, and putting on the mind of Christ.
- We can have victory in our **bodies** as we understand that our body is a temple of the Holy Spirit and that we need to govern what we put into it.

Learning from Experiences

Our victory also depends upon our experiences and what we learn from them. Our failures are great teachers of victory. The Bible teaches that *a good man falls seven times but gets up each time.* Every time he gets up is a victory in his life, leading to ultimate victory in life.

PRAYER

Heavenly Father, in the name of Jesus, I thank You for the provision You have made for my victorious living. Thank You for giving me all the great and precious promises for victory in my life. I receive Your promises of walking in faith and victory daily.

Thank You, Father, for giving me victory over all stumbling blocks, and I will walk victoriously over all the challenges and issues before me. Thank You for Your concern in every area of my life, knowing that nothing is too small or too hard for You. My victory is in You as I walk in obedience to Your Word.

In Jesus' name. Amen.

1 John 5:4
"For whatever is born of God overcomes the world. And this is the victory that has overcome the world—our faith."

WISDOM

Proverbs 8:10-11
"Receive my instruction, and not silver; and knowledge rather than choice gold. For wisdom is better than rubies, and all the things that may be desired are not to be compared to it."

The Value of Wisdom

In my estimation, wisdom is knowing all things. As human beings, we are limited in our thinking and in our strength. We are also limited in our aspirations; however, we are taught that wisdom is above any product or material thing, indicating that wisdom is a spirit.

Wisdom is a force that we cannot see and cannot touch, yet it is incredibly real. We know when we have wisdom, and others can identify when we exercise wisdom in our lives. Wisdom will guide us into everything good. There is only one person who is all-knowing and all-powerful, and that is God Himself.

Wisdom in Creation

In the Book of Proverbs, wisdom is described as *crying out*, which means it has a voice. Wisdom teaches sensitivity and perception. It is written that wisdom was with God from the beginning, and God used wisdom when He created the heavens, the earth, and mankind. What a source of power, innovation, and creativity—sustaining beyond and above time.

Wisdom Freely Given

God has not limited wisdom to Himself. We learn in **James 1:5**: *"If any of you lack wisdom, let him ask of God, that gives to all men liberally, and upbraids not; and it shall be given to him."*

If we ask God for wisdom, He will give it to us liberally and will not hold back. When God created man, He took a part of Himself and placed it inside of us. When God breathed into man, He breathed into man everything He was and everything He had. He made us in His image and likeness.

Our level of wisdom is lower than His because He is our Creator. However, the portion God has given to man is able to sustain him and give him the vantage point of being above every situation and circumstance.

The Power of Wisdom

Wisdom gives us knowledge that we cannot learn from books or experience.

- Wisdom leads and wisdom guides.
- Wisdom gives insight and foresight into any and every situation.
- Wisdom is not limited by our abilities or restricted by time.
- Wisdom is not limited by nationality or personal background.

Wisdom is freely given to anyone who takes the time to pursue it. Anyone who seeks out and obtains knowledge of what is around them can access wisdom.

Wisdom will share information, knowledge, foresight, and insight with whoever asks and with whoever takes the time to seek it.

Calling Upon Wisdom

Today is our opportunity to make the quality decision to call upon wisdom in every situation that concerns us. Call upon wisdom to govern our lives and our thoughts. Call upon wisdom to govern our families, our businesses, and everything we are involved in. Wisdom will lead and direct us and give us victory.

PRAYER

Heavenly Father, in the name of Jesus, I thank You today that You give wisdom freely to all who ask. I ask, in the name of Jesus, for the spirit of wisdom to fall upon me, to lead me, and to guide me into victory in my life.

My mind is set on obtaining all the wisdom necessary to live a victorious life. I pray that wisdom will give me insight and foresight above and beyond my wildest dreams.

I thank and praise You and magnify Your great name today and every day.

In the name of Jesus. Amen.

Proverbs 4:7-8
"Wisdom is the principal thing; therefore get wisdom: and with all your getting, get understanding. Exalt her, and she shall promote you; she shall bring you to honor when you embrace her."

WORSHIP GOD

John 4:23-24
"But the hour comes, and now is, when the true worshippers shall worship the Father in spirit and in truth: for the Father seeks such to worship Him. God is a Spirit, and they that worship Him must worship Him in spirit and in truth."

The Meaning of Worship

Worship is giving honor and praise to someone greater than yourself. Worship is choosing to demonstrate your affection toward someone with higher power and status than yourself—someone above you, someone who has control over every situation.

Worship is reserved for deity—a supernatural being far above us mortals and who has no needs that we can provide. The only service we can offer is worship. The One who stands in all might and power, the Creator of the entire universe, the one true and living God—He alone deserves our worship.

Why God Deserves Our Worship

He deserves our worship for who He is—the great and mighty God, all-sufficient in Himself. Nothing and no one can add to Him to make Him greater. No one can contribute anything to make Him better. He is entirely sufficient in Himself. He controls everything in this universe. Our response and acknowledgment of His greatness and power is to worship Him.

We are called to worship Him as part of our lifestyle. He is the One who created us. He is the One who holds our next breath in His hands. He is the Only One who has created all things good and right for us. The benefits of His creation should lead us to thank Him and appreciate Him. We express thanksgiving and appreciation to God Almighty by worshiping Him.

God's Unchanging Nature

Everything around us deteriorates, but God never does. He is constant. He is infinite. His greatness is so profound that we must look up to Him. As we look up, we recognize how finite we are, which compels us to bow down and worship His greatness.

Despite our flaws and frailties, we are often disappointed and disappointing. There is no disappointment or second-guessing with God. He is infinite, great, and powerful. Submitting to Him is an act of worship. He is God, and we are His subjects. As His created beings, we bow, honor, and reverence the Creator. As God, our Creator, all our worship goes to Him—not only as an act of our free will but because He deserves it.

PRAYER

Heavenly Father, in the name of Jesus, I worship You. I reverence You, I honor You, and I thank You for being the great and mighty God that You are. Thank You, Father, that You never change. Your love, Your mercy, and Your compassion toward me never change.

I bow in reverence and worship You for all Your goodness, Your love, and all the benefits You have orchestrated for Your children to enjoy. Today and every day, receive my worship. Receive the honor, respect, and appreciation in my heart for who You are. I will give You glory, honor, and praise every day.

In Jesus' name. Amen.

Matthew 4:10
"Then said Jesus unto him, 'Get thee hence, Satan: for it is written, Thou shalt worship the Lord thy God, and Him only shalt thou serve.'"

ENDORSEMENTS

BY PASTOR PAULA WHITE-CAIN

Dear Friends,

I cannot express enough how highly I recommend this Daily Devotional, especially for those seeking encouragement, renewed strength, and hope in their everyday lives.

I have had the privilege of knowing Elder Marguerite for many decades. She has been a steadfast pillar at the City of Destiny in Apopka, Florida, since my calling as Senior Pastor. To this day, "in season and out of season," she remains unwavering in her commitment to her calling. Through all the trials and triumphs of parish life, she has stood firm, embodying truth and love in a world that often feels broken and uncertain.

Two remarkable qualities make her Daily Devotional a true source of nurturing spirituality. First, it is indeed "Devotional," reflecting the author's own deep devotion. Elder Marguerite is entirely sold out to the Lord! I have witnessed her faithfulness through personal grief, challenging circumstances, and the ebbs and flows of life. Her unwavering spirit is a gift that we all need, and this book is infused with that very essence.

Secondly, it is "Daily" — a continuous source of inspiration. Like the well that never runs dry, this devotional will sustain you, even in the midst of drought or the relentless heat of life's challenges. I encourage you to read it for a year and then start all over again; you will find it just as refreshing each time.

So, here it is: Marguerite Remy-Esannason's Daily Devotional. Is it a hidden gem, waiting to be uncovered beneath the sands of your busy life? Perhaps. Is it a Stream of Living Water, ready to quench your thirst during the long days? Absolutely! Embrace it and let it nourish your spirit and soul.

Thank you, dear Elder Marguerite, for your unwavering commitment to sharing these precious truths.

- *Pastor Paula White-Cain*

BY REVEREND DR. PAUL ZAHL

Elder Marguerite's Devotional *Life*. I italicize "*Life*" because it is her life, and her honest-to-God daily ministry, that breathe *life* into her Daily Devotions. Elder Marguerite's Devotions are breathed into by the Holy Spirit of God because she herself lives a "breathed-into" life.

Now I'm not saying that she herself is the Breath of God. But I am saying that her heart, her mind and her life-purpose are submitted to God, and therefore her one-on-one interactions -- and therefore her written reflections -- are 'intubated' by the Breath of God. ["Take My Breath Away" (Berlin, 1986)]

Elder Marguerite (Esannason) didn't start out this way, or at least, not exactly. (Tho' she had a good beginning with loving Christian parents and family.)

She was a successful businesswoman -- most highly regarded both in the USA and in Canada. She was married to wonderful Fred (Esannason) and cared for him with unfailing, prayerful solicitude right up to the day he died. She was a founding Elder of City of Destiny (now Story Life Church) in Apopka, Florida. And she has mentored numberless Christian women, especially younger single Christian women, through thick and thin. She is also a consistent prayer partner to faithful Sisters and Brothers all over the world. I think that for everything she "touches", she becomes a kind of *Atlas*, bearing its hopes before God upon her utterly altruistic shoulders.

Her Devotions reflect -- or rather, express -- her confidence in God. The "issues" facing 'Elder M', as I call her in lasting friendship and regard, are not pushed down, nor fictionally minimized. But nor are they ever the last word. She places them before God -- the God of our Bible, mighty to save and persisting in Love to the end -- and thus they are transformed. The reader's problems are transformed.

So "read, mark, learn and inwardly digest" these Daily Devotions. They come from a Spiritual Warrior of superb uncommon Biblical faith.

P.S. Every time I am able to be with 'Elder M' in person, I come away, refreshed, well fed (in every sense), and ready to put on the Whole Armor of God. So, dear Reader, get ready: "Up Up and Away" (5th Dimension, 1967)!

- Reverend Dr. Paul Zahl

Made in the USA
Coppell, TX
06 January 2026